TOP 10 FLASHPOINTS IN STUDENT RATINGS
AND THE EVALUATION OF TEACHING

Other books by Ronald A. Berk

Available from Stylus Publishing

Thirteen Strategies to Measure College Teaching
Humor as an Instructional Defibrillator
Professors Are From Mars®, Students Are From Snickers®

Available from other publishers

Top Secret Tips for Successful Humor in the Workplace
The Five-Minute Time Manager for College Students
A Guide to Criterion-Referenced Test Construction
Performance Assessment: Methods and Applications
Educational Evaluation Methodology: The State of the Art
Handbook of Methods for Detecting Test Bias
Criterion-Referenced Measurement: The State of the Art
Screening and Diagnosis of Children with Learning Disabilities
DeGangi-Berk Test of Sensory Integration Manual

TOP 10
FLASHPOINTS
in Student Ratings and
the Evaluation of Teaching

What Faculty and Administrators Must Know
to Protect Themselves in Employment Decisions

RONALD A. BERK
Foreword by Wilbert J. McKeachie

> *Flashpoint:* a critical stage in a process, trouble spot, contentious issue, volatile hot button, or lowest temperature at which a flammable liquid will give off enough vapor to ignite.

> **WARNING:**
> *This book contains humor, which may not be suitable for some of you, particularly if you have the sense of humor of a kumquat. But that's okay. To compensate for your "serious" perspective, this book is closed captioned for the Humor-Impaired. After each attempt at jocularity, the punch line will be explained in ( ) so that you can laugh along with the rest of us.*

Sty/us

STERLING, VIRGINIA

Published by Stylus Publishing, LLC
22883 Quicksilver Drive
Sterling, Virginia 20166-2102

Library of Congress Cataloging-in-Publication Data
Berk, Ronald A.
   Top 10 flashpoints in student ratings and the evaluation
of teaching : what faculty and administrators must know to
protect themselves in employment decisions / Ronald A.
Berk ; foreword by Wilbert J. McKeachie.
   p.   cm.
Includes bibliographical references and index.
ISBN 978-1-57922-980-1 (cloth : alk. paper)
ISBN 978-1-57922-981-8 (pbk. : alk. paper)
ISBN 978-1-57922-982-5 (library networkable e-edition)
ISBN 978-1-57922-983-2 (consumer e-edition)
   1. Student evaluation of teachers.   2. College teachers—
Rating of.   3. College teaching—Evaluation.   I. Title.
II. Title: Top ten flashpoints in student ratings and the
evaluation of teaching.
LB2333.B473   2013
371.14'4—dc23   2012044328

13-digit ISBN: 978-1-57922-980-1 (cloth)
13-digit ISBN: 978-1-57922-981-8 (paper)
13-digit ISBN: 978-1-57922-982-5 (library networkable
e-edition)
13-digit ISBN: 978-1-57922-983-2 (consumer e-edition)

Bulk Purchases

Quantity discounts are available for use in workshops
and for staff development.
Call 1-800-232-0223

First Edition, 2013

10   9   8   7   6   5   4   3   2   1

To *Sadie Grace Anna Heiliger,*
one of my hilarious granddaughters

CONTENTS

ACKNOWLEDGMENTS

Writing a book of this height, width, girth, BMI, density, hue, and blood glucose and cholesterol levels is a piece of chocolate cake. Not really. Actually, it requires a place to write, an author who is heavily medicated (kidding), a few supportive colleagues, and the expertise of a publication team that can turn a manuscript into a polished book.

The head of that team is my publisher *John von Knorring* of Stylus Publishing, who has a clear appreciation of my twisted mind, I think. This is my fourth book with Stylus. John truly understands the value of strategically placed humor in books on "serious" topics. The humor can help emphasize, anesthetize, and accessorize the meaning of the serious message. I am also extremely grateful to my managing production editor *Alexandra Hartnett* and copy editor *Amy Chamberlain* for their meticulous work and special care of my manuscript through the most critical stages of the publication process. I still learn so much about writing from my editors.

Despite the efforts of these professionals in the production of this book, there may be substantive and editorial errores or omis sions. None of these people is responsible. Ultimately, there is only one person who should be held totally accountable for the mistakes in this book, and that person, of course, is Jimmy Kimmel.

I thank *Bill McKeachie* for his vote of confidence and willingness to write the Foreword. For the opening parody on the history of student ratings, I received valuable feedback from *Raoul Arreola, Bill Pallett, Mike Theall,* and an anonymous student-ratings expert. They reviewed the skimpy facts, such as names, dates, statistics, and publications, reported in an earlier version of that chapter. I'm also appreciative to have a good buddy like *Mike Theall,* who is always responsive to any of my requests on technical topics and provides continuous support, friendship, and a whacky sense of humor. I thank *Maxine Gilling* for pointing me toward the Scriven and Stufflebeam definitions of "evaluation" in the pre-flashpoint on terminology. Also, I solicited reactions to my choices of flashpoints and received very creative ideas from Mike, *Ed Nuhfer, Trav Johnson,* and *Amy Gross,* and Mike and

Ed's suggestions for other flashpoints were very helpful. In fact, I have enough flashes bursting in my head to generate another Top 10.

The original inspiration for the flashpoints was two keynote addresses I gave on faculty evaluation at medical education conferences in Kuala Lumpur, Malaysia, and Riyadh, Saudi Arabia in spring of 2012. There were very encouraging audience responses to the five flashpoints (they appear as Flashpoints 1 through 5 in this book). I am grateful to conference directors *Ronald Harden* and *Pat Lilley* (Kuala Lumpur) and *Ahmad Al-Shafei* (Riyadh) for giving me the opportunities to present at those conferences.

After those presentations on five flashpoints, I added another five flashpoints. They were derived largely from the spirited discussions and lively debate among practitioners of faculty evaluation on the Internet listserv sponsored by the Professional and Organizational Development (POD) Network in Higher Education. I scoured the discourse posted from 2010 to 2012 to extract the most confusing, misunderstood, contentious, and thorny issues on the topic, the issues that appear over and over again. I am grateful to the regular contributors for sustaining that discourse with their reflective insights and probing, sometimes vexing, questions. They included *Alan Bender, Nira Hativa, Kevin Johnston, Mick La Lopa, Linda Nilson, Ed Nuhfer, Lynn Sorenson*, and *Mike Theall*. There were oodles of other occasional contributors to those discussions: *Victoria Bhavsar, Dakin Burdick, Eric Grosse, Kevin Guidry, Barbara Hornum, Trav Johnson, Bruce Larson, Angela Linse, Patricia McGee, David Nelson, Ross Peterson-Veatch, Ken Sagendorf,* and *Richard Tiberius*.

This book also meant a commitment by me to continue writing. I am blessed to be in a profession that has required me to write and publish, whether I felt like it or not, and extremely grateful to a dozen highly skilled and patient copy editors who have tried their best to mold me into a writer. Since retiring from Johns Hopkins 6.833 years ago, I have been trying to sustain my writing at my pre-retirement pace. The race has been close. There's nothing like competing against yourself. One of the Rons should win!

The difference in writing as a "retiree" is that I can peck away at my keyboard in my home office while in my skivvies, munching on ~~Cheez-Its~~ celery sticks (yuck!) with peanut butter, and sipping my flavored java, at least some of the time. At other times, outside my home I create temporary offices with my PC plopped on top of out-of-date magazines on end tables just about everywhere: doctors' offices, emergency rooms, and surgical waiting rooms for interminable periods, airline terminals, auto repair shops, and coffee shops. I get more writing and editing done in these venues than you can possibly imagine.

Finally, I owe my family a 14-point, bold, uppercase **THANK YOU** for their support: my amazing wife *Marion*; my incredible daughters, *Boo Boo* (aka *Marissa*) and *Cori* (aka *Corinne*); my terrific, thoughtful son-in-law *Chris*; my most loving, cute, and hilarious granddaughters *Ella, Sadie,* and *Macy* (aka *Baby Boo*); and my *Mommy,* who at 94 years old is still sharp and who supports everything I produce, especially the humor. My family provides me with endless sources of joy, laughter, and inspiration. Without these blessings in my life, this book would be meaningless.

FOREWORD

I n the past few years there have been a number of very good articles about the evaluation of teaching in colleges and universities. Ron Berk's *Top 10 Flashpoints* pulls together the latest and best research and writing in this field in a very helpful and humorous guide for administrators, faculty, and scholars in the field. Each of Ron's 10 flashpoints deals with a serious issue that is much argued in faculty meetings and among administrators. For each flashpoint, Ron defines the issue, reviews the options available, and then provides recommended solutions.

Those who read the entire book will end up with a much more sophisticated understanding of the problems in evaluating college teaching as well as a helpful guide to possible solutions. Those who have specific problems or questions not only will find useful answers but also will gain a clearer sense of the theories and research that underlie the answers.

I have been doing research on and reading and writing about the evaluation of teaching for more than 60 years. Nonetheless, I learned a great deal from this book. I recommend it to all faculty, administrators, and scholars in the field.

Wilbert J. McKeachie
Professor Emeritus
University of Michigan

INTRODUCTION

> **FLASHPOINT:** a critical stage in a process, trouble spot, contentious issue, volatile hot button, or lowest temperature at which a flammable liquid will give off enough vapor to ignite.

If you've read any of my previous books, you know I've given off clouds of vapor. For you language scholars, *flashpoint* is derived from two Latin words, *flashus*, meaning "your shorts," and *pointum*, meaning "are on fire."

Why Flashpoints?

This book is not another review of the research on student ratings or user's manual on how to evaluate teaching effectiveness. That was my previous book. This one is a *state-of-the-art update of research and its implications for practice,* primarily since 2006 (Arreola, 2007; Berk, 2006; Seldin & Associates, 2006), *with specific targets:* the flashpoints that have emerged as critical issues, conflicts, discordant topics, and intractable problems in the evaluation of teaching effectiveness. They are the most prickly, thorny, vexing, and knotty topics that most every administrator and professor must confront. "Ouch! I just vexed myself."

These flashpoints cause confusion, misunderstanding, dissension, hand-to-hand combat, and, ultimately, inaccurate and unfair decisions about faculty. Although there are many more than 10 issues in this percolating cauldron of controversy, there are certain flashpoints that seem to pop up over and over again, on listservs, LinkedIn group discussions, and blogs and in articles, books, and teaching conference programs (Berk, 2012). Plus, they generate a firestorm of debate among faculty and administrators. This contribution is an attempt to decrease some of that percolating and popping.

Problem-Based Writing (PBW)

If you are currently using any instrument to measure teaching performance in face-to-face (f2f), blended/hybrid, or online courses, then you are probably struggling with one or more flashpoints. This book is a consumer's guide to trouble-shooting these flashpoints. It is written expressly for faculty and administrators who don't have the time to fool around (on the job) hunting down solutions. I do the hunting so you don't have to. I don't want to waste your time or my words.

The motto of this book is "Get to the flashpoint and the solution." This is the inauguration of my new PBW series on *problem-based writing.* Your problems are the foci of my writing. The structure of each chapter will be governed by the PBW perspective:

1. *Definition:* Each flashpoint will be succinctly defined.
2. *Options:* The options available based on research and practice will be described.
3. *Recommended solution:* Specific, concrete, evidence-based recommendations for faculty and administrators will be proffered to move them to action.

There doesn't seem to be any shortcut, quick fix, or multilevel marketing scheme to improve the quality of teaching. Hopefully, tackling these flashpoints head-on will be one positive step toward that improvement. If this step helps, perhaps another volume covering more flashpoints will be produced. I'm probably already working on those flashpoints as you're reading this paragraph. I've noticed a tendency for flashpoints to reproduce by themselves, which is kind of scary.

Top 10 Flashpoints

The "Top 10 Flashpoints" are (1) student ratings versus multiple sources of evidence; (2) sources of evidence versus decisions (which come first?); (3) quality of "home-grown" rating scales versus commercially developed scales; (4) paper-and-pencil versus online scale administration; (5) standardized versus unstandardized online scale administration; (6) low online-administration response rates; (7) global items versus total scale ratings; (8) scoring "neutral," "not applicable," "not observed," and blank answers; (9) criterion-referenced versus norm-referenced rating interpretations; and

(10) face-to-face versus online course rating scales. The first three relate to critical decisions about the scales and sources of evidence chosen, the next three address scale administration issues, and the final batch covers score interpretation options and the choice of scales for online courses. *All 10 conclude with recommended evidence-based practices according to professional and legal standards to protect faculty and administrators in employment decision making.* Those standards, which have been ignored by most administrators, will be described in Flashpoints 1, 7, and 9.

How to Read the Flashpoints

As you have already guessed, this is not a cover-to-cover, sit-down or stand-up reader to take with you to the beach or the ski slope, skydiving, rock climbing, shark fishing, or on any similar leisure activity. It's a guide to problem solving.

Step 1. Pick a problem that's driving you nuts.
Step 2. Go to the appropriate chapter.
Step 3. Read only those sections that interest you until you have a grasp of the issues.
Step 4. Ruminate over the options and my recommendations.
Step 5. Take action on whatever has to be done; that's what counts.

Read as little as possible. After all, that's what your students would do. For example, if you are charged with evaluating your online courses, go to Flashpoint 10 (chapter 12), check out the options, then make a decision on what scale would be a "best buy."

Preparing for the Flashpoints

Before tackling any of the 10 flashpoints, I recommend that you brace yourself for the rough terrain and speed bumps ahead. This is serious, life-changing material, like the brain-altering, disease-preventing, diabetes-reversing programs aired during the semi-annual PBS fund-raising drives every two weeks. Yeah, *right!* What better way to prepare you for this material than expose you first to *a hefty dose of humor* on a topic near and dear to your heart: the history of student rating scales. Cardiac-wise, what topic could possibly be more hilarious?

So much has been published on rating scales that there has to be a smidgen of space to squeeze in a parody for my first chapter. Is it possible to cover the entire history and inject some of my twisted humor along the journey? You bet. Of course, you can skip it and proceed straight to "Flashpoint World." Your choice. I hope you enjoy the parody.

A FRACTURED, SEMI-FACTUAL HISTORY
OF STUDENT RATINGS OF TEACHING
A Parody

U sually the history of any serious topic triggers the gag reflex in most nonhistorians. However, this topic is different from most. Gagging isn't an option. Over the past few years, there have been incendiary debates over student rating forms, online administration procedures, global items, low response rates, and rating use and interpretation over loads of listservs, social-media group discussions, journal articles, books, professional blogs, and other media.

Introduction

The reverberations of these debates have been felt on college campuses as far away as Pandora University, where the topic has provoked the verbal equivalent of an *Avatar*-scale firefight. Rather than fan the flames of this combustible metaphor, I thought this introductory chapter could provide a time-out, a refreshing break from this contentious topic for all faculty and administrators, before delving into the serious "flashpoints" up ahead. It also may shed some energy-saving light—like those corkscrew-shaped bulbs—on how this situation evolved, with an emphasis on practical implications.

"Rocky and Bullwinkle" Approach

Do any of you remember "Fractured Fairy Tales" on *The Rocky and Bullwinkle Show*? NO? What about Boris and Natasha? What were you *doing*? Oh well, it doesn't matter, my youngin' academic readers. This chapter is written in the same spirit as that politically satirical cult cartoon, except without the politics, cult, and cartoon. It is a parody, with the bonus of actual events in the history of student ratings—kind of a print mockumentary. You'll even get a few morsels of content within its humorous context. (*FACT ALERT*: Most of the names, dates, book and scale titles, and survey statistics are correct. Plus, they have been verified, notarized, and pasteurized by the accounting firm of Arreola, Theall, Pallett, and Seldin, LLP.)

Laughter Outcomes

There are two primary outcomes for this chapter: (1) to give you a grasp of the significant academic activities, research, publications, and major players in the unfolding student ratings debate; and (2) to provide you with a sense of what these contributions and their applications mean for you in your teaching or administrative position. There is also one physiological outcome: to elicit a chuckle or two, maybe a guffaw, as you process the major events.

If you laugh, I hope you will experience one of these physical signs: (a) burst your guts, (b) rupture key internal organs, (c) wet yourself, or (d) spurt your latté or green tea through your nostrils and all over your keyboard. Anything less will be disappointing. (*NOTE:* Many of the references along my path through history have been omitted to permit more space for jokes, plus you will Google them anyway if you're interested further. Please refer to the chapters that follow and to Berk [2006] for those references and lots more jokes.)

A Metaphorical Cul-de-Sac

There is more research on student ratings than any other topic in higher education. The evaluation of teaching has been in a metaphorical cul-de-sac with *student ratings as the universal barometer of teaching performance*. And if you've ever been in a cul-de-sac or a metaphor, you know how weird that can be. Only recently has a trend developed toward using multiple sources of evidence and better metaphors that don't have dead ends or involve hectopascals.

So how in the ivory tower did we get ~~into this mess~~ to this point? Let's trace the major historical events. Hold on to your global items or, better yet, discard them (see Flashpoint 7). Here we go.

A Fractured History of Student Ratings

This history covers a timeline on the "Student Ratings" Facebook page of approximately 100 billion years, give or take a day or two, ranging from the age of dinosaurs to the age of sleazy, tawdry, insipid reality TV programs about the private lives of "celebrities" with specious talent. Obviously, it's impossible to shoehorn every event that occurred during that period in this chapter. Instead, the entire span is partitioned into seven major eras, and key student-ratings activities within each are highlighted.

Meso-Concussion Era

A long time ago, at a university far, far away, there were no student rating scales. During prehistoric times, there was only one university, near present-day Detroit (Me, 2003), which was actually more like a community college because research and the four-year liberal arts curriculum hadn't been invented yet. This institution was called Cave University, named after its major donor, Harold University (Me, 2005).

Students were very concerned about the quality of teaching back then, just as three or four of your students are now. In fact, they created their own method of evaluation to express their opinions. For example, if an instructor (a) strayed from the syllabus, (b) fell behind the planned schedule, (c) used think-pair-share or otherwise tried to engage students, (d) wrote faulty test items, or (e) cut class to watch one of those *Jurassic Park* movies (which he—they were all men—inevitably regretted), the students would club him (Me & You, 2005). This produced lots of bumps on the heads of instructors and loads of concussions, like those experienced by NFL quarterbacks wearing football helmets, which prompted historians to call this period the *Meso-Concussion Era*.

Admittedly, this practice seemed a bit crude and excessive even at the time, but it held faculty accountable for their teaching, plus it promoted a steady flow of patients through the ER and, eventually, the development of teaching helmets made out of tree stumps. Obviously, there was no need for tenure because there was so much faculty turnover, as word of the clubbings and the really bulky helmets spread all the way to Grand Rapids, which was on the land currently occupied by Wyoming.

That takes us up to 1923. I skipped over 90 billion years because nothing happened that was relevant to this review.

Meso-Remmers Era

Between 1923 and 1959, student rating practices began. The first graphic rating scale for teachers was developed in 1923 by psychologist Max Freyd in Vienna, Austria. Wait, that's the wrong Freud. The one in Austria had a "u." Sorry. This Dr. Freyd defined *successful teaching* in terms of sense of humor, neatness in dress, tact, patience, and other attributes. He lasted one year as a professor at the University of Pennsylvania, which is in Vienna, Virginia, before moving into private industry.

Freyd's article on his rating scale was followed by the work of Herman Remmers, who lasted more than one year at Purdue University, also in Vienna, Virginia, home of the Pittsburgh Penguins. He and his colleague George Brandenburg, composer of the "George Concerto," designed the *Purdue Rating Scale for Instructors.* In the late 1920s and 1930 Remmers and Brandenburg were the authors of early publications on the *Purdue Scale,* related to its reliability, relationships to student grades and alumni ratings (see References), and later, factor analysis (Smalzried & Remmers, 1943). They found 10 traits, such as personal appearance and personal peculiarities. The *Purdue Scale* is the forerunner of the *Purdue Instructor Course Evaluation Service (PICES)* developed in the 1970s, which is now administered online, more than 80 years after the original was created (see Flashpoint 4).

As a tribute to Dr. Remmers's contributions, these years were named the *Meso-~~Penguins~~Remmers Era.* Dr. Remmers pretty much owned it. His pioneering work on student ratings also led to his recognition as "HH Cool R Rating Man." WROOONG! That's a rapper. Dr. Remmers's real title is "Father of Student Evaluation Research." Now I suppose you're going to shout out, "Who's the mother?" Are you ready for the answer? It's "Foxy" Bubble Answer-Sheet. Mrs. Answer-Sheet was a descendant from a high stack of Answer-Sheets. And that wraps up this 36-year era.

Meso-Boomer Era

The 1960s were rocked by student protests on campuses, the Vietnam War, Woodstock, hallucinogens, and the Broadway musical *Hair* (based on the TV program *The Brady Bunch*). This "boomer" generation was blamed for just about everything during this period, known as the *Meso-Boomer Era.* These boomers demanded that college administrators give them a voice in educational decisions that affected them, such as the food in the cafeteria. They expressed their collective voice, not always on key, by singing social-commentary folk songs like "Puff" while sitting in the entrances to administration buildings, as well as writing and administering rating scales to their classes to evaluate their instructors. They even published the ratings in student newspapers so students could use them as a shopping guide to course selection. This idea stuck and 50 years later can be considered the forerunner of the RateMyProfessor.com online ratings site, where you can find the "Hottest Professors."

During this period there were few centrally administered rating systems in universities to evaluate teaching effectiveness. Most uses of student ratings by faculty were voluntary. In general, the quality of the scales available was dreadful, and their use as evaluation tools was fragmented, unsystematic, and arbitrary, kind of like this chapter. As for research, there was only a dash; all was quiet on the publication front. The researchers were busy in the reference section of their university libraries preparing for the next decade and waiting for Google to be invented.

Meso-Burgeon Era

The 1970s were called the "Golden Age of Student Ratings Research," in tribute to a bunch of "senior" professors who were doing research while living in assisted learning communities. The research on the relationships between student ratings and instructor, student, and course characteristics burgeoned during these years, named the *Meso-Burgeon Era*. As the evidence for the validity and reliability of scales mounted, the use of the scales increased and spread across the land, beyond East Lansing, Nebraska (home of the Maryland Tar Heels).

During these years, the term *student evaluation of teaching* (*SET*) appeared in a few research publications instead of the more widely used *student rating scale*. *SET* became a misnomer for the form administered to students. Later, *SET* grew an additional letter *E* to become *SETE*, which stood for *student evaluation of teaching effectiveness*. Sometimes *SEI* (or *student evaluation of instruction*) was preferred. Near the end of the decade, we were all excited to hear that researchers were not going to change the acronym *SETE* to *FUTON* (see chapter 2, Flashpoint Terminology, for details).

One of the most prominent researchers during this era was Herbert Marsh, now at the University of Oxford, in Cambridge. He began a series of studies on student rating scales in the mid-'70s that finally ended in 2000 (see References). The bulk of his publications on technical issues focused on the scale he developed: *Students' Evaluations of Educational Quality (SEEQ)*.

Speaking of *SEEQ*, several commercially produced, nationally normed student rating scales hit the academic marketplace during this era (see Flashpoint 4). Their superior technical quality compared to many "home-grown" tools and their electronically generated custom report forms provided colleges with the option of shopping for their rating scales. The first two scales were *SIR* in 1972 (Educational Testing Service) and *IDEA* in 1975 (Kansas State University). *IAS Online* (University of Washington) and *SEEQ* (Centre for Educational Assessment, Perth, Western Australia) became available later.

Student-rating item banks also grew during the '70s. Those banks permitted faculty to withdraw statements from a catalog in order to deposit them into their own customized scales. Two of these banks were ~~FDICs~~ *PICES* in 1974 (Purdue University), mentioned previously, and *CIEQ* in 1977 (University of Arizona). However, entering this commercial rating scale derby was not without challenges. Most ventures lacking a pronounceable, catchy three- to five-letter acronym tanked immediately.

These burgeoning years also witnessed the first major wave of books on the topic. The winning prize for first book went to Richard Miller for *Evaluating Faculty Performance* in 1972. He also took the silver medal with *Developing Programs for Faculty Evaluation* in 1974. The bronze went to Ken Doyle for his 1975 work on student evaluations, aptly titled *Student Evaluation of Instruction*. This was followed in 1979 by John Centra's *Determining Faculty Effectiveness*, which synthesized all the earlier work and proffered guidelines for future practices.

At the end of the decade, one survey found that 55% of liberal arts college deans always used student ratings to evaluate teaching performance for decisions about contract renewal and promotion and tenure. However, only a tiny 10% conducted any research on the quality of their scales. These statistics were reported just in the nick of time before the next paragraph.

Meso-Meta Era

The 1980s were really booooring! The research continued on a larger scale, and statistical reviews of the studies (aka meta-analyses) were conducted by such authors as Cohen (1980, 1981) and Feldman (1989a, 1989b). Of course, this period had to be labeled the *Meso-Meta Era*. In 1980 Peter Seldin of Pace University in upstate Saskatchewan published his first of thousands of books on the topic, *Successful Faculty Evaluation Programs*. Ken Doyle produced his second book on the topic, *Evaluating Teaching*, in 1981. (Are you still awake?)

The administration of student rating scales spread throughout the lymph nodes of academe. By 1988 their use by college deans spiked to 80%, with still only a paltry 14% of deans gathering evidence on the technical aspects of their scales. Faculty members were blissfully unaware that faulty, technically putrid rating scales were probably being used as the sole data source for decisions about their careers and lymph nodes. The continued poor quality of the scales left faculty and administrators vulnerable to litigation on violations of federal antidiscrimination laws (see Flashpoint 7) and numerous node-spreading diseases. That takes us to—guess what? Oops, I forgot.

Meso-Pumped Era

The 1990s were like a nice, deep breath of fresh gasoline, which was $974.99 a gallon at the pump ($974.00 for cash only, $972.99 with a carwash, $970.50 with tire pressure check, $985.99 with FREE 37-point safety inspection for an additional $49.95). They are hereafter referred to as the *Meso-Pumped Era*. Little did anyone anticipate how this era would be trumped at the pump by the first years of the new millennium and up to the present day with even higher gas prices.

After all this pumping, the use of student rating scales spread to Kalamazoo (known to tourists as "The Big Apple"), and faculty finally began to complain about their validity, reliability, and overall value for decisions about promotion and tenure (the scales, that is, not the tourists). This was not unreasonable, given the lack of attention paid to the quality of scales over the preceding 90 billion years (see Flashpoint 3).

<<<*WEATHER ALERT*: I interrupt this section to warn you of impending wetness in the next three paragraphs. I'm not kidding. Although I'm not a meteorologist, I know things. You might want to don appropriate apparel. Don't blame me if you get wet. You may now rejoin this section, already in progress. *END OF ALERT.*>>>

This debate intensified throughout the decade with a torrential downpour of publications challenging and contributing to the technical characteristics of the scales, particularly a series of articles by William Cashin (see References) of the IDEA Center at Kansas State University, which was temporarily located in New Hampshire, and a 1990 edited work by Mike Theall and Jennifer Franklin titled *Student Ratings of Instruction*. As part of this debate, another steady stream of research flowed toward using additional strategies to measure teaching effectiveness, especially peer ratings, self-ratings, videos, alumni ratings, interviews, student performance, teaching scholarship, and teaching portfolios (see Flashpoint 2).

This stream leaked into books by John Centra (*Reflective Faculty Evaluation*, 1993), Larry Braskamp and John Ory (*Assessing Faculty Work*, 1994), Peter Seldin (*Improving College Teaching*, 1995), and Raoul Arreola (the first and second editions of *Developing a Comprehensive Faculty Evaluation System*, 1995, 2000) and into an edited volume by Seldin and Associates (*Changing Practices in Evaluating Teaching*, 1999). In 1997 a special issue of the *American Psychologist* was devoted exclusively to studies of student ratings of teaching and contained major contributions by Wilbert McKeachie, Gerald Gillmore, Herbert Marsh, and others. They created a confluence of valuable resources for faculty and administrators to use to evaluate teaching. With this flood of publications and additional meta-analysis studies by d'Apollonia and Abrami (1997a, 1997b, 1997c), the technical evidence was mounting.

This cascading trend was also being reflected increasingly in practice. Although use of student ratings peaked at 88% by the end of the decade, peer (46%), administrator (65–70%), and self (61–82%) ratings were rising over the rapids of teaching performance, as my liquid metaphor was dropping off to a trickle (see Flashpoint 2). Both faculty and administrators were realizing the limitations of student ratings for teaching improvement and important career decisions (see Flashpoint 1).

Meso-Online-Everything Era

The first decade of the new millennium rode on the search engines of the previous decade. A bunch of publications kicked it off with a half-dozen edited volumes on student ratings and faculty evaluation published by Jossey-Bass in their *Teaching and Learning* series (Ryan, 2000, #83; Lewis, 2001, #87; Knapper & Cranton, 2002, #88; Sorenson & Johnson, 2004, #96) and in *Directions for Institutional Research* (Theall, Abrami, & Mets, 2001, #109; Colbeck, 2002, #114).

There were no planet-shattering technical developments, but there were several software options created specifically for online administration and reporting of student rating scales. Only an occasional drip (oops! sorry—residual fluidity from the previous metaphor) of articles on midterm formative ratings and other topics appeared.

Finally, three books hit the Amazon website in the last half of the decade: Arreola's (2007) 48th edition of his popular work, Seldin's (2006)

128th edited volume, and our hero's psychometric-humorous attempt (Berk, 2006). Shortly thereafter, a monograph on student ratings research that was sponsored by the Higher Education Quality Council of Ontario, located in Vienna at the time, was written by Pamela Gravestock and Emily Gregor-Greenleaf (*Student Course Evaluations: Research, Models and Trends,* 2008). Is there redundancy among these sources? There is some; however, they were written from different perspectives. But nobody will ever know for sure, because it's unlikely anyone will plow through all four books, even though they are definitely worth the plowing.

Most of the activity and discourse on student ratings during this period concentrated on practical issues. There were several trends that continued from the previous decade:

1. Student ratings data were being supplemented with other data, particularly peer review of teaching and course materials, teaching portfolios, and letters of recommendation by the professors' mommy or daddy, for summative decisions (see Flashpoints 1 and 2).
2. Administrators and faculty reviewed the quality of their tools to consider either using a commercial package, such as *THOUGHT* from the MIND Center in Biloxi, Georgia, or developing their own "home-grown" scales (see Flashpoint 4).
3. The technical quality of many "home-grown" scales prompted me to coin the new psychometric term *putrid* (see Flashpoint 3).
4. Their lack of growth led to the label "Peter Pan scales."
5. The debate over paper-based versus online scale administration raged with the factors of cost and low student response rates as the deal breakers (see Flashpoints 4 and 6).
6. Global items grew in popularity for use in summative decisions about faculty, despite their inappropriateness for those decisions (see Flashpoint 7).

The interest in online everything increased significantly by the end of the decade, which justified naming this the *Meso-Online-Everything Era.* In fact, several vendors hit up a bunch of ivory towers to provide "online delivery services" for student rating scales, including CollegeNET, ConnectEDU, EvaluationKITS, and IOTA Solutions. These businesses supplied online administration to hundreds of institutions worldwide (see Flashpoint 4).

The importance of response rates to the validity of students' ratings became a critical factor in decisions to adopt online systems (see Flashpoint

6). Other validity issues related to biases in ratings and the veracity of ratings were studied (see Flashpoint 1). As academicians entered 2011, the question of what scales to use for online and blended/hybrid courses remained unanswered by most directors of distance education programs and others (see Flashpoint 10).

Meso-Flashpoint Era

The preceding decade spilled over into constant debate and discussions on the POD (Professional and Organizational Development Network in Higher Education) Listserv and other listservs and blogs about loads of issues, which have become the "flashpoints" of this book. The range of topics, the levels of confusion and misunderstanding, the disturbing practices revealed, and the number of arguments over procedures and interpretations have broken all records, Guinness-wise. Further, there has been a disproportionate amount of attention and even obsession with student rating scales compared to all the other sources of evidence except peer review and teaching portfolios.

The questions that keep sprouting up about the factors that influence student-ratings interpretation have coincided with two timely reviews of the literature: one by Stephen Benton and William Cashin (2012), still at the IDEA Center, and an edited monograph by Mary Kite (2012), prepared for the Society for the Teaching of Psychology website and sponsored by Dr. Phil. The latter review did consider topics beyond student ratings, such as online courses, course portfolios, peer review, and couples with serious relationship issues. As we skip along through this decade, there is no sign that the sprouting will be stopping. At this stage, there are few options other than flashpointing.

Epilogue

Well, there it is. I bet you're thinking, "History, schmistory. What was *that* all about?" Despite this cutesy romp through Student-Ratings World and a staggering 873 books and thousands of articles, monographs, conference presentations, and blogs on the topic, some behaviors remain the same. For example, even today, the mere mention of *teaching evaluation* to many college professors triggers mental images of the shower scene from Hitchcock's *Psycho*, complete with Norman Bates's butcher knife, Marion Crane's blood-curdling screams, and the shower curtain ripped from the hooks, with blood swirling down the drain in black-and-white. The professors were thinking in color: "Why not just beat me now rather than view my online student ratings (which I now get lickety-split, thanks to speedy electronic processing)?" Hmmm. Kind of sounds like a prehistoric concept to me (a little *Meso-Concussion déjà vu*).

Despite the progress made, with deans, department heads, and faculty moving toward multiple sources of evidence for formative and summative decisions, student ratings are still virtually synonymous with teaching evaluation and are asynchronously administered to students worldwide, and also on a few planets to which Microsoft has outsourced most of its software and services since closing down India for technical repairs. (*PARAGRAPHUS INTERRUPTUS:* What's with that sentence? It is sooo long and complicated. My editor calls it a "conjunctive, double-breasted diphthong." I'm not sure why.) Student ratings remain the most influential measure of performance used in promotion and tenure decisions at institutions that emphasize teaching effectiveness.

For now, many faculty and administrators are still using "home-grown" scales that do not meet basic professional and legal standards. This makes institutions prone to committing serious mistakes in faculty contracts, promotion, and tenure, especially when administrators use normed student ratings to rank faculty for those decisions (see Flashpoint 9). In fact, the use of these scales in hiring, promotion, demotion, or firing of any instructor can violate federal antidiscrimination laws related to pay, gender, age, race, ethnicity, and other protected categories (see Flashpoint 7); and faculty and administrators may not even be aware of these violations. Commercially developed scales may also violate these laws, particularly on the "80/20 rule" for adverse impact (see Flashpoint 9). Bummer! Ya think we have work to do? Uh-huh.

In the meantime, it is incumbent on everyone involved in the evaluation of teaching to understand the value of student rating scales and what they can contribute to that evaluation process. However, it is also critical to appreciate their limitations and consider multiple sources of evidence in decision making (see Flashpoints 1 and 2). Their popularity notwithstanding, maybe their ubiquity will serve higher education better in the next *Meso-WhoKnowsWhat Era*, when I update this schmistory.

2

FLASHPOINT TERMINOLOGY
Student Evaluation of Teaching (SET) vs. Student Rating Scale

Before we tackle the next 10 flashpoints, we need to clarify terminology. As faculty, administrators, and researchers have written on the topic of student ratings, their perspectives and disciplines have influenced the terms they use. The greatest confusion involves student evaluation of teaching, *or* SET. *It is a misnomer for* student rating scale *in the context of professional standards in measurement and evaluation.*

Use of the Term *Student Evaluation of Teaching* (*SET*)

Since the 1970s, several researchers adopted the term *SET* in their publications, but most use *student rating scale* (*student ratings*) to refer to the form administered to students. That dichotomy in terminology has continued for 40 years. Over that time period, *SET* grew an additional letter *E* to become *SETE*, which we all know is like a small sofa. (Sorry, a little furniture humor.) Actually, *SETE* stood for *student evaluation of teaching effectiveness*. Sometimes *SEI* (*student evaluation of instruction*) was preferred.

Now, *SET*, *SETE*, and *SEI* appear in teaching and evaluation journals and, occasionally, in listserv discussions, blogs, books, and football tailgating parties. Even a few pundits on the topic use those acronyms. A variation on *SET* is also part of the ERIC database descriptor "student evaluation of teacher performance."

What's the Problem?

Who cares? Why is this terminology such a problem? After all that we have learned about this topic, it seems reasonable that we should be meticulous about the terms we choose in professional discourse, especially in refereed publications on the research and in tailgating. In all the acronyms—*SET*, *SETE*, and *SEI*—the culprit is the first *E*. "Evaluation" ascribes a process or specific use of ratings to a *single scale*. I suspect that many academicians use *evaluation* as a generic term rather than as a professional one for the context in which it is being applied. The problem is that there isn't one definition in the literature on evaluation that even comes close to the meaning or intent of any of the terms represented by those acronyms. Let's review the "Top 10" definitions of *evaluation* in the most powerhouse sources I was able to dig up.

Top 10 Definitions of *Evaluation*

The word *evaluation* is derived from two French words, *éval*, meaning "shish," and *uàtion*, meaning "kabob your colleague." The 10 definitions that follow were drawn from publications of the experts on evaluation and the products of joint committee deliberations by professional associations over thousands of years on professional standards for measurement and evaluation practices in the United States. The concepts and processes described should clarify the terminology used throughout this book.

First, consider a few definitions by experts:

1. [Evaluation:] "the *process* of determining the merit, worth, or value of something, or the product of that process" (Scriven, 1991, p. 139)
2. [Evaluation:] "the *collection and analysis* of quality information for decision makers" (Stufflebeam & Shinkfield, 2007, p. 3)
3. [Evaluation:] "*systematic process* of delineating, obtaining, reporting, and applying descriptive and judgmental information about some object's merit, worth, probity, feasibility, safety, significance, or equity" (Stufflebeam & Shinkfield, 2007, p. 698)

Here are definitions from the U.S. Joint Committee on Standards for Educational Evaluation for *Program Evaluation Standards*:

4. [Evaluation:] "*systematic investigation* of the worth or merit of an object" (Joint Committee on Standards for Educational Evaluation, 1994, p. 3)

5. [Evaluation:] *"systematic investigation* of the value, importance, or significance of something or someone along defined dimensions" (Yarbrough, Shulha, Hopson, & Caruthers, 2011, p. 287)

The following definitions are from the U.S. Joint Committee on Standards for Educational Evaluation for *Personnel Evaluation Standards*:

6. [Evaluation:] *"systematic investigation* of the worth or merit of an evaluatee's qualifications or performance in a given role in relation to a set of expectations or standards of performance" (Joint Committee on Standards for Educational Evaluation, 2009, p. 195)
7. [Personnel evaluation:] *"systematic assessment* of a person's performance and/or qualifications in relation to a professional role and some specified and defensible institutional purpose" (Joint Committee on Standards for Educational Evaluation, 2009, p. 3)

The American Evaluation Association also offers a rather comprehensive definition:

8. [Evaluation:] *"assessing* the strengths and weaknesses of programs, policies, personnel, products, and organizations to improve their effectiveness" (American Evaluation Association, 2012)

Finally, in *Standards for Educational and Psychological Testing,* the AERA (American Educational Research Association), APA (American Psychological Association), and NCME (National Council on Measurement in Education) Joint Committee on Standards defines *program evaluation* and *assessment* as follows:

9. [Program evaluation:] *"collection and synthesis* of systematic evidence about the use, operation, and effects of some planned set of procedures" (AERA, APA, & NCME Joint Committee on Standards, 1999, p. 180)
10. [Assessment:] *"systematic method* of obtaining information from [scales] and other sources, used to draw inferences about characteristics of people, objects, or programs" (AERA, APA, & NCME Joint Committee on Standards, 1999, p. 172)

What's the Point?

I don't have a clue. I got lost in all of those definitions and the jargon. However, as you perused the definitions, I bet you couldn't miss the *italicized* words. Those operative words in almost every case were *systematic process, investigation, method*, or something close. It doesn't matter whether the target of the evaluation is personnel or a program; a systematic process or collection of evidence or information is involved. Further, that process usually determines the *worth*, or value, of the target.

When "intensity" (Strongly Agree–Strongly Disagree), "frequency" (Always–Never), or "quantity" (All–None) anchors are used on the rating scale, the students are neither "evaluating" teaching nor "determining its worth or value"; they also do not "investigate" or "collect evidence." They *supply* evidence by simply responding to items on a scale, similar to answering items on a test. Their responses translate their opinions about specific teaching and course characteristics into "ratings."

If the rating scale contains items with "evaluation" (Effective–Ineffective or Excellent–Poor) or "comparison" (More–Less [than other courses]) anchors, students are judging worth or value. This is also true of global ratings (Excellent–Poor) of a professor or course (see Flashpoint 7). Arreola (n.d.) also made this distinction between "ratings" and "evaluation" for global items.

Overall, in these various applications students are rating general and specific behaviors they have observed in class and/or online. They do not actually engage in an evaluation process, as the definitions require, although their judgments using "evaluation" and "comparison" anchors come close. Their role is to provide data from their observations for the evaluators to use in making decisions. Benton and Cashin (2012) perceptively observed that

> Using the term "rating" rather than "evaluation" helps to distinguish between the people who provide the information (sources of data) and those who interpret it (evaluators) in combination with other sources of information. (p. 1)

For student rating scales, the data are supplied by students and used by the evaluators who are professors and administrators.

Recommendations

Moratorium on SET, SETE, and SEI

In the context of personnel decisions about faculty, which is what this book is all about, the terms containing "evaluation," as well as the related acronyms *SET, SETE*, and *SEI should be abandoned* as misnomers for "student rating scales." They are misleading and totally inappropriate in the contexts in which they are being used.

I respectfully request that the use of those terms in professional discourse of any kind be prohibited, especially by journal editors in their guidelines for author submissions. I recommend that anyone caught using one of those terms or photographed speeding in a work zone, even when nobody is visibly working, be fined for the first offense or placed in overnight lock-up on *Law & Order*. Ha-ha. The Acronym Police (AP) are watching. Don't even think about a second violation.

The issues to be thrashed out in the upcoming flashpoints address the characteristics and psychometric properties of the scales, their administration procedures, and the use and interpretation of ratings for formative, summative, and program decisions. The ratings may also be used in conjunction with the ratings and scores from other measures in the process of evaluating teaching effectiveness.

Conclusion

The evaluations based on multiple sources of evidence are conducted by professors and administrators (Berk, 2006), not by students. It is the processes of *personnel evaluation* and *assessment,* as defined in the *Personnel Evaluation Standards* and *Standards for Educational and Psychological Testing,* respectively, that permit several different sources of appropriate evidence to be collected for the purpose of decision making. *Student rating scales represent one measure and generate just one source of information, or data, in those processes.*

FLASHPOINT 1
Student Ratings vs. Multiple Sources of Evidence

Student rating scales have dominated as the primary or, more often, the only measure of teaching effectiveness in colleges and universities worldwide and on a few remote planets. This state of practice is contrary to the advice of a cadre of experts and regardless of the limitations of student input for comprehensively evaluating teaching effectiveness. Several other measures should be used in conjunction with student ratings.

Role of Student Ratings

Student rating scales have been the primary measure of teaching effectiveness for the past 50 years. Students have had a critical role in the teaching-learning feedback system. Their input in formative and summative decision making by means of their ratings has been recommended on an international level (Griffin & Cook, 2009; Strategy Group, 2011; Surgenor, 2011).

As the parody in chapter 1 so hysterically conveyed, over the past 100 billion years more has been written on this topic in higher education than any other. To date, there are *nearly 2,000 references* on the topic (Benton & Cashin, 2012), with the *first journal article published 90 years ago* (Freyd, 1923). In fact, in higher education there is more research on and experience with student ratings than all the other measures of teaching effectiveness combined (Berk, 2006). However, if you fast-forward 10 paragraphs, you will find 14 other measures. That's tankers of research. If you need to be brought up to speed quickly with the research on student ratings, check out these up-to-date, easily accessible reviews (Benton & Cashin, 2012; Gravestock & Gregor-Greenleaf, 2008; Kite, 2012).

With this incredible volume of scholarly products and practice in academia, you would think that student ratings would be the ideal—not to be confused with *IDEA*—solution for evaluating teaching effectiveness. Ubiquity-wise, student ratings is on top. So what's the problem?

What's the Problem?

There are three major limitations to using only student ratings for decision making: (1) students' qualifications as raters, (2) waning validity evidence, and (3) inadequacy as a source of evidence for decision making. Let's look at these limitations.

Students' Qualifications as Raters

As informative as student ratings can be about teaching, there are numerous *behaviors and skills that define teaching effectiveness* that students are *not qualified to rate*, such as a professor's knowledge and content expertise, teaching methods, course design and organization, use of technology, quality of course materials, assessment instruments, grading practices, and sartorial taste (Ali & Sell, 1998; Calderon, Gabbin, & Green, 1996; Cashin, 1989; Cohen & McKeachie, 1980; Coren, 2001; d'Apollonia & Abrami, 1997a; Green, Calderon, & Reider, 1998; Hoyt & Pallett, 1999; Kieg & Waggoner, 1994; Marsh, 2007; Ory & Ryan, 2001; Svinicki & McKeachie, 2011; Theall & Franklin, 2001).

YIIIKES! What's left that students *can* measure? They can provide feedback at a certain level in most of those areas, but it will take peers and other qualified professionals, such as a Savile Row tailor, to rate those skills in depth. There is so much to measure, but it should be completed only by those individuals who are in the best position to provide the information.

Waning Validity Evidence

The validity of student ratings has also been challenged by Nilson (2012) in three areas: (1) relationship between student ratings and learning; (2) sources of bias in the ratings, including professor's charisma, physical attractiveness, personality, gender, age, rank, and class length (also see Addison & Stowell, 2012; Basow & Martin, 2012); and (3) accuracy and veracity of the ratings, especially in the context of online administrations. In reviewing the validity studies of yesteryear (i.e., 1970s and 1980s) compared to the more recent wave of research findings, Nilson concluded that *evidence substantiating the validity of student ratings has diminished significantly*, and its usefulness in decisions about faculty should be reexamined. When your validity is waning, that can't be good. Certainly, further scrutiny of recent studies is warranted to confirm or disconfirm Nilson's conclusion.

Inadequate Source of Evidence for Decision Making

Based on these possible limitations and weaknesses, student ratings can provide only one portion of the information needed to infer teaching effectiveness, one piece of the lemon meringue pie. (Sorry, I'm getting hungry.) Yet, unfortunately, that's pretty much all that's available at most institutions. When those ratings alone are used for decision making, the decisions will have been based on incomplete and biased evidence.

Without additional evidence of teaching effectiveness, *student ratings can lead to incorrect, unfair, and evil career decisions about faculty* that can affect their contract renewal, annual salary increase, professional development, and promotion and tenure (Wines & Lau, 2006). Yet, administrators' pushing to use only student ratings for these decisions continues unabated. Even discriminatory practices based on age, gender, race, ethnicity, and other protected classes may occur, knowingly or unknowingly, because of these scales (U.S. EEOC, 2010) (see Flashpoints 7 and 9 for further details). The bottom line: *Student ratings from well-constructed scales are a necessary, but not sufficient, source of evidence for comprehensively evaluating teaching effectiveness.*

Multiple Sources of Evidence

Since the 1990s the practice of augmenting student ratings with other data sources of teaching effectiveness has been gaining traction in liberal arts colleges, medical schools/colleges (Berk, 2012), and other institutions. Such sources can serve to *broaden and deepen the evidence base* used to evaluate courses and the quality of teaching (Arreola, 2007; Benton & Cashin, 2012; Berk, 2005, 2006; Braskamp & Ory, 1994; Cashin, 2003; Gravestock & Gregor-Greenleaf, 2008; Hoyt & Pallett, 1999; Knapper & Cranton, 2001; Ory, 2001; Seldin, 2006; Theall & Feldman, 2007; Theall & Franklin, 1990).

In fact, several comprehensive models of "faculty evaluation" that include multiple sources of evidence have been proposed (Arreola, 2007; Berk, 2006, 2009b; Braskamp & Ory, 1994; Centra, 1993; Gravestock & Gregor-Greenleaf, 2008). Some models attach greater weight to student and peer ratings and less weight to self, administrator, and alumni ratings and other sources. All of these models can be used to arrive at formative and summative decisions.

15 Sources of Evidence

Ah-ha! Did you peek at these sources nine paragraphs back? I saw you. You can fool me on some pages, but not on all. At least you're here now. Guess what?

There are 15 potential sources of evidence of teaching effectiveness: (1) student ratings, (2) peer classroom observations, (3) peer review of course materials, (4) external expert ratings, (5) self-ratings, (6) videos, (7) student interviews, (8) exit and alumni ratings, (9) employer ratings, (10) mentor's advice, (11) administrator ratings, (12) teaching scholarship, (13) teaching awards, (14) learning outcome measures, and (15) teaching (course) portfolio.

Berk (2006) describes several major characteristics of each source, including the type of measure needed to gather the evidence, the person(s) responsible for providing the evidence (i.e., students, peers, external experts, mentors, instructors, or administrators), the person or committee who uses the evidence, and the decision(s) typically rendered based on that data (i.e., formative, summative, or program). Our hero also critically examined the value and contribution of these sources for measuring teaching effectiveness based on the current state of research and practice. His latest recommendations will be presented in Flashpoint 2. (*MYSTERY QUESTION:* Berk's book covers 13, not 15. So what's the difference? One of the strategies is split into items 2 and 3 here, and item 10 was added. *MYSTERY SOLVED.*)

Triangulation

There are gobs of articles that weigh the merits and shortcomings of these various sources of evidence (Berk, 2005, 2006). Put simply: *There is no perfect source or combination of sources.* Each source can supply unique information but is also fallible, sinful, and evil, usually in ways different from the other sources. For example, the unreliability and biases of peer ratings are not the same as those of student ratings; student ratings have other weaknesses (Nilson, 2012).

What you should do: ~~First, you might consider early retirement.~~ Since no single source can light up the sky with fireworks, *draw from three or more different sources of evidence,* where the *strengths of each source can compensate for weaknesses of the other sources,* thereby *converging on a decision about teaching effectiveness that is more accurate and reliable than one based on any single source* (Appling, Naumann, & Berk, 2001). The explosion of three sources will work. (*TIME-OUT:* Wow! I'm out of breath from that long sentence, which structurally is called a "carnivorous carbuncle," and excited about the rocket's red glare and bombs bursting in air. Now, *this* is getting interesting.) This notion of *triangulation* is derived from a compensatory model of decision making and the pyrotechnic images of the Zambelli fireworks I still remember.

Nuhfer (2010) argues that the evaluation of teaching is a fractal form with extensive neural networks and, therefore, far too complicated to be measured with any single source. Given the complexity of measuring the act of teaching in a real-time classroom environment, online virtual class, or hybrid-time class, it is reasonable to expect that *multiple sources can provide a more accurate, reliable, and comprehensive picture of teaching effectiveness than just one source.*

Standards for Quality

According to *Standards for Educational and Psychological Testing* (AERA, APA, & NCME Joint Committee on Standards, 1999), the role of each source should be clearly explicated before combining the different sources (Standard 14.13). For example, if student ratings are weighted more heavily than self and peer ratings (Berk, Naumann, & Appling, 2004), the rationale and weighting procedure should be defined. Further, the decision maker should *integrate the information from only those sources for which validity evidence is available* (Standard 14.13). The quality of the sources chosen should be beyond reproach technically.

Research Evidence

Because there hasn't been an adequate number of documented experiences with multiple sources, there is a scarcity of empirical evidence to support the use of any particular combination of sources (e.g., Barnett, Matthews, & Jackson, 2003; Stalmeijer, Dolmans, Wolfhagen, Peters, van Coppenolle, & Scherpbier, 2010; Stehle, Spinath, & Kadmon, 2012). There are also only a few surveys of the frequency of use of individual sources (Barnett & Matthews, 2009; Seldin, 1999). Research is needed on various combinations of measures to determine "best practices" for different decisions.

Recommendations

All experts on faculty evaluation recommend multiple sources of evidence to evaluate teaching effectiveness. They may not all agree on which sources, but that's okay. Although some of these experts are riding Harleys on country roads or sitting in beach chairs somewhere, sipping mind-altering beverages as they enjoy their retirement, their psychometric position on multiple sources has been officially certified by Dr. Oz, who recommends taking buckets of homeopathic remedies for which there is barely any research support. How compelling is that? I know—maybe not so much. (*NOTE:* Their lack of agreement on specific sources may be attributable, at least in part, to the effects of their beverages or other substances. After all, they're boomers and traditionalists.)

Complementary Multiple Sources

So what are you supposed to do? Beyond student ratings or retirement, is it worth the extra effort, time, cost, and aggravation to develop the additional measures suggested in this section? Just what new information do you have to gain for decision making?

As those instruments are being built, it should become clear that they are intended to measure different teaching behaviors that contribute to teaching effectiveness. Each measure should bite off a separate chunk of behaviors from the lemon meringue pie a few paragraphs back. They should be designed to be complementary, not redundant; however, some overlap of behaviors may be justified for corroboration purposes.

There is even research evidence on the relationships between student ratings and several other measures that supports their complementarity. (*DERIVATION:* The word *complementarity* is derived from 17 words from various dead languages, such as French, which I have forgotten.) Benton and Cashin's (2012) research review reported the relationships between student ratings and ratings from observers, self, alumni, and administrators, which were low to moderate. That means there are lots of new information and insights on teaching to be gained by tapping those additional sources of evidence.

[*FOR RESEARCHERS ONLY:* Here are the actual validity coefficients with student ratings: trained external observers (.50 with global ratings), self (.30–.45), alumni (.54–.80), administrators (.47–.62; .39 with global ratings).]

Conclusion

Now you have the green light to pursue multiple sources with your faculty to evaluate teaching effectiveness. You better hurry because we are approaching a red-light-camera intersection, and I don't want another ticket. *Obtain the commitment of your faculty to the specific sources in order of priority* and form a small, but amazingly qualified, bevy of brilliant faculty (5 to 10 members) to take the leadership on building a multisource model that will dazzle the next team of on-site accreditation reviewers. More details on these steps will be given in the recommendations for Flashpoint 2.

4

FLASHPOINT 2

Sources of Evidence vs. Decisions: Which Come First?

Rating scales are administered and then confusion typically occurs over what to do with the results and how to interpret them for specific decisions. A better strategy would be to do exactly the opposite of that practice—spin your head around 180°, Exorcist-style. The type of decision should drive the selection of the appropriate sources of evidence, the types of data needed for the decision, and the design of the report form. Custom-tailor the sources, data, and form to fit the decision. The information and format of the evidence a professor needs to improve his or her teaching are very different from that required by a department chair for annual review (for contract renewal or merit pay) or by a faculty committee for promotion and tenure review. The sources of evidence and formats of the reports can either hinder or facilitate the decision-making process.

Types of Decisions

According to Seldin (1999), *teaching is the major criterion in assessing overall faculty performance in liberal arts colleges* (98%), compared to student advising (64%), committee work (59%), research (41%), publications (31%), and public service (24%). Although these figures may not hold up for research universities and community colleges, teaching didactic and/or clinical courses is still a critical job requirement and a criterion on which most faculty members are evaluated.

There are two types of *individual decisions* in faculty evaluation that are guided by the *Personnel Evaluation Standards* (Joint Committee on Standards for Educational Evaluation, 2009), plus one decision about *programs*, which follows the *Program Evaluation Standards* (Yarbrough et al., 2011). You may already be familiar with these decisions in the context of student assessment. However, decisions about faculty relate to employment or personnel issues. Many of the standards governing those decisions are different from those about students.

Formative Decisions

A formative decision is a type of decision faculty make *to improve and shape the quality of their teaching.* It is based on evidence of teaching effectiveness they gather and use to plan and revise their teaching semester after semester (or quarter after quarter). These decisions may be made by the professor alone or with the guidance of a trusted colleague or mentor. Most of the information gathered is analyzed confidentially.

Timely, accurate, and relevant *feedback* of the results from different rating scales (e.g., student, peer, self, or video) can be used for teaching improvement. Even better, *consultative feedback* by faculty developers, peers (trained or untrained), or graduate students can lead to greater changes (Marincovich, 1999; Penny & Coe, 2004). Multiple sources of evidence can identify teaching problems, aid in the design of improvement strategies, and determine follow-up steps to improve teaching.

This evidence can be collected, the decisions rendered, and the subsequent adjustments in teaching completed at any time during the course. Some of these decisions allow the students to benefit from those changes while they are taking the course; others will occur after the course, as the professor prepares for the next semester.

Summative Decisions

Summative decisions are made by the administrative-type person who controls a professor's destiny and future in higher education. This individual may be the dean, associate dean, program director, department head or chair, or emperor/empress in residence. This administrator gathers evidence of a professor's teaching effectiveness along with other evidence, such as scholarship, clinical practice, service, and old or dead relatives with enormous vats of money. A department chair may also become a source of evidence by rating the professor on *indirect contributions to the instructional program,* such as learning environment, curricular development, and mentoring other faculty on teaching improvement (Hoyt & Pallett, 1999) and professionalism related to teaching. *All this evidence is used to "sum up" his or her overall performance to decide about contract renewal or dismissal, annual merit pay, teaching awards, faculty development, and promotion and tenure.*

Although promotion and tenure decisions are often made by a faculty committee of high-ranking superstars, a letter of recommendation by the dean is typically required to reach the committee to initiate the review process. These summative decisions are *high-stakes, possibly final, employment decisions* (if tenure is involved), executed at different points in time to determine a professor's progression through the ranks and success—or not—as an academician.

Program Decisions

Several sources of evidence can be used for program decisions also. These decisions relate to *the curriculum, admissions and graduation requirements, and program effectiveness.* They are *not* individual decisions; instead, they focus on *products and processes.* The evidence usually is derived from various types of faculty and student input and output and employers' performance appraisal of students on the job during internships and as graduates. It is also collected to provide documentation to satisfy the criteria for accreditation review and to bulk up the self-study.

What's the Problem?

The problem is to match the best sources of evidence of teaching effectiveness to the decisions that need to be made. The pool of available sources must be evaluated for their quality and quantity. You may need another pool or additional sources. Then the challenge is to pick the most appropriate and highest quality sources for the specific decision. *The decision should drive the choices of evidence.* Think carefully about the decision in terms of the time frame, conditions, information needed, and the personnel or programs about which the decision will be made.

Matching Sources of Evidence to the Decision

Consider all the sources of evidence currently available based on the research and experiences of others (Berk, 2006). Which ones seem to be most appropriate for your decisions? Prioritize the sources before you begin the task of collecting the evidence, which may involve the design and construction of new measures.

As a jump-start to your selection of sources, you can use my review of the aforementioned 15 sources of evidence of teaching effectiveness (Berk, 2005, 2006, 2009b). Here are my top picks, based on the literature, for formative, summative, and program decisions:

FORMATIVE DECISIONS

- Student ratings
- Peer classroom observations
- Peer review of course materials
- External expert ratings
- Self-ratings
- Videos
- Student interviews
- Mentor's advice

SUMMATIVE DECISIONS (ANNUAL REVIEW FOR CONTRACT RENEWAL AND MERIT PAY)

- Student ratings
- Self-ratings
- Teaching scholarship
- Administrator ratings
- Teaching portfolio (for several courses over the year)
- Peer classroom observations (report written expressly for summative decision)
- Peer review of course materials (report written expressly for summative decision)
- Mentor's review (progress report written expressly for summative decision)

SUMMATIVE DECISIONS (PROMOTION AND TENURE)

- Student ratings
- Self-ratings
- Teaching scholarship
- Administrator ratings
- Teaching portfolio (across several years' courses)
- Peer review (report written expressly for summative decision)

- Mentor's review (progress report written expressly for summative decision)

PROGRAM DECISIONS

- Student ratings
- Exit and alumni ratings
- Employer ratings

You probably noticed one particular source among the potential 15 that was conspicuously omitted from all of my recommended sources: learning outcome measures, or student performance. This is a flashpoint in itself and beyond the scope of this book. Suffice it to say for now: Isolating students' course achievement at one point in time or their gains over time that are attributable directly to teaching is nearly impossible (Berk, 2006). The complexity increases considerably when attempting to compare faculty who teach different courses with different students and measures. It would be extremely difficult to defend student performance as a valid source of evidence of teaching effectiveness for any decision.

The multiple sources that were recommended previously for each decision can be configured into the *360° multisource feedback (MSF) model* of assessment (Berk, 2009a, 2009b) or other model for accreditation documentation of teaching evaluation. The sources for each decision may be added gradually to the model. This is an ongoing process for your institution.

Recommendations

So now that you've seen my picks, which sources are you going to choose? So many sources, so little time! Which sources do you already have? What is the quality of your measures used to provide evidence of teaching effectiveness? Are all faculty stakeholders involved in the current process?

Six Steps to Choose Your Sources

You have some decisions to make, starting with "Where do I begin?" That's the same question asked by a guy who was getting ready to eat a rhinoceros. Here are a few suggestions:

1. ~~What part of the rhino do you like best? The tusk.~~ *Assemble your small faculty committee.* As recommended in the previous flashpoint, hand-pick appropriate committee members, including at least one professor with expertise in measurement and evaluation (they usually hang around education, psychology, and sociology departments).

2. *Map the outcomes for the semester (or quarter) and year.* Discuss a plan of attack. What are the highest priorities? Consider whether accreditation review is on the horizon or somewhere else. That could change the priorities. Consider the following ideas for a plan of action.

3. *Start with student ratings.* Consider the content and quality of your current scale and determine whether it needs a minor or major tune-up for the decisions being made. Decide what has to be done and who will do it.

4. *Review the other sources of evidence* with your faculty to decide the next steps. Which sources will your faculty embrace as reflecting best practices in teaching? Weigh the pluses and minuses of the different sources. Prepare options for your faculty presentation. Then duck.

5. *Decide which combination of sources is best* for your faculty. Identify which sources should be used—although prepared differently—for both formative and summative decisions, such as self and peer ratings, and which sources should be used for one type of decision but not the other, such as administrator ratings and teaching portfolio.

6. *Design a detailed plan to build those sources,* one at a time, to create an evaluation model for each decision (see Berk, 2009b). Delegate responsibility for and ownership of the various tasks involved. This is when the individual commitment to "put it on the line" counts. Remember: Administrators do not have time for these steps. They just need the data that faculty have agreed to use for decision making about you.

Conclusion

Whatever combination of sources you choose to use, take the time and make the effort to design the scales, administer the scales, and report the results appropriately. *The accuracy of faculty evaluation decisions depends on the integrity of the process and the validity and reliability of the multiple sources of evidence you collect.* This endeavor may seem rather formidable, but keep in mind that you are not alone in this process. Your colleagues at other institutions are probably struggling with the same issues. Maybe you could pool resources or medications to get through it.

5

FLASHPOINT 3

Quality of "Home-Grown" Rating Scales vs. Commercially Developed Scales

Many of the rating scales developed by faculty committees in colleges and universities do not meet even the most basic criteria for psychometric quality required by professional and legal standards. Most of the scales are flawed internally and administered and interpreted incorrectly, and rarely is there any evidence of rating reliability and validity. The serious concern is that decisions about the careers of faculty are being made with these scales.

Quality Control

R esearchers have reviewed the quality of student rating scales used by colleges and universities throughout the United States and Canada (Abrami, 2001; Arreola, 2007; Berk, 1979, 2006; d'Apollonia & Abrami, 1997b, 1997c; Franklin, 2001; Franklin & Theall, 1990; Gravestock & Gregor-Greenleaf, 2008; Hoyt & Pallett, 1999; Ory & Ryan, 2001; Seldin, 1999; Theall & Franklin, 2000). The instruments are either commercially developed scales with predesigned reporting forms or "home-grown," locally constructed measures usually built by faculty committees. The former exhibit the professional quality control of the company that developed the scales and reports, such as Educational Testing Service and the IDEA Center (see Flashpoint 4); the latter have no consistency in the development process and rarely any formal procedures for controlling psychometric quality.

What's the Problem?

The problem is the lack of quality control for "home-grown" scales, which may very well extend to institutions worldwide. It could be *due to a lack of commitment, importance, accountability, or interest; inappropriate personnel without the essential skills; or limited resources.* No one knows for sure. Regardless of the reason, the picture is ugly. If your scale is ugly, you're not alone.

Weaknesses of "Home-Grown" Scales

Reviewers of practices at institutions in North America have found the following problem areas in, or weaknesses of, "home-grown" scales:

- poor or no specifications of teaching behaviors and course characteristics;
- faulty items (statements and anchors);
- ambiguous or confusing directions;
- unstandardized administration procedures;
- inappropriate data collection, analysis, and reporting;
- inappropriate interpretation or misuse of ratings;
- no adjustments in ratings for extraneous factors;
- no psychometric studies of score reliability and validity; and
- no guidelines or training for faculty and administrators to use the results correctly for appropriate decisions.

Does the term *putrid* summarize current practices? How does your scale stack up against these problems? Fertilizer-wise, many "home-grown" scales are lacking. Their development is arrested. They are more like "Peter Pan scales."

Negative Consequences of Poor Quality

The potential negative consequences of using faulty measures to make biased and unfair decisions can be devastating (Wines & Lau, 2006). Moreover, this evaluation addresses the quality of student rating scales only. What would be the quality of peer observations, self-ratings, and administrator ratings and their interpretations? Serious attention needs to be devoted to the quality control of all "home-grown" scales.

From a broader perspective, *poor quality scales violate U.S. testing/scaling standards* according to the *Standards for Educational and Psychological Testing* (AERA, APA, & NCME Joint Committee on Standards, 1999), *The Personnel Evaluation Standards* (Joint Committee on Standards for Educational Evaluation, 2009), and the U.S. Equal Employment Opportunity Commission's (EEOC) *Uniform Guidelines on Employee Selection Procedures* (U.S. Code of Federal Regulations, 1978). The psychometric requirements for instruments used for summative, employment decisions about faculty are rigorous and appropriate for their purposes (see Flashpoints 7 and 9 for details).

Recommendations

This issue reduces to the leadership and the composition of the faculty committee that accepts the responsibility to develop the scales and reports and/or the external consultant or vendor hired to guide the development process.

Committee Composition

The psychometric standards for the construction, administration, analysis, and interpretation of scales must be articulated and guided by professionals trained in those standards (AERA, APA, & NCME Joint Committee on Standards, 1999). As Flashpoint 2 emphasizes, if the committee does not contain one or more professors with expertise in psychometrics, then it should be ashamed of itself. That is a prescription for putridity and the previous list of problems and other forms of alliteration. Reviewers rarely found anyone with these skills on the committees of the institutions surveyed.

Faculty Development on Item Writing

All faculty members should be given workshops on item writing and scale structure. "Why?" you query. Because faculty cannot avoid writing scale items. In the development process of the student rating scale as well as other scales, they will be *reviewing, selecting, critiquing, adapting, and writing items.* Even if faculty are excellent test item writers, that doesn't mean they can write scale items.

The structure and criteria for scale items are very different from those for test items (Berk, 2006)—not difficult, just different. Even with commercially developed instruments, *professors are usually given the option to add up to 10 course-specific items*; in other words, they *will* need to write items. Rules for writing scale items are available in references on scale construction (Berk, 2006; DeVellis, 2012; Dunn-Rankin, Knezek, Wallace, & Zhang, 2004; Netemeyer, Bearden, & Sharma, 2003; Streiner & Norman, 2008).

6

FLASHPOINT 4

Paper-and-Pencil vs. Online Scale Administration

The battle between paper-and-pencil and online administration of student rating scales is still being fought on many campuses worldwide. Despite an international trend and numerous advantages and improvements in online systems over the past decade, there are faculty who still dig their spurs and heels in and a bunch of institutions that have resisted the conversion. Much has been learned about how to increase response rates (Flashpoint 6) and how to overcome many of the deterrents to adopting an online system. Online administration, analysis, and reporting can be executed in-house or by an out-house vendor specializing in that processing.

Comparison of Paper-and-Pencil and Online Administration

A detailed examination of the advantages and disadvantages of the two modes of administration according to 15 key factors has been presented by Berk (2006). Surprise, surprise! There are major differences between them. Although both are far from perfect, *the benefits of the online mode and the improvements in the delivery system with the research and experiences over the last few years were found to exceed the pluses of the paper-based mode.* Furthermore, most Net Geners don't know what a pencil is. Unless it's an iPencil, it's not on their radar or part of their mode.

COMMERCIAL BREAK

Speaking of modes, as a Southwest Airlines flight was getting ready to take off, the flight attendant said the following:

"Please turn off all electronic equipment now. The following are unacceptable for your cell phone:

A. low-volume mode,
B. vibrate mode,
C. airplane mode, or
D. hide-it-from-the-flight-attendant mode."

Don't ya just love Southwest?

We now resume this flashpoint, already in progress.

Benefits of Online Mode

The benefits of the online mode include *ease of administration, administration flextime, low cost, rapid turnaround time for results, ease of scale revision, and higher quality and greater quantity of unstructured responses* (Anderson, Cain, & Bird, 2005; Berk, 2006; Heath, Lawyer, & Rasmussen, 2007; Liu, 2006; Sorenson & Johnson, 2003).

Problems With Online Mode

There are several problems with online administration: (a) students' concerns, (b) low response rates and negative bias in those responses, (c) lack of standardized administration, (d) scale response bias, and (e) lower ratings compared with paper-and-pencil versions. These problems are addressed in this chapter or by other flashpoints.

Students' concerns about *lack of anonymity, confidentiality of ratings, inaccessibility, inconvenience, and technical problems* have been addressed at many institutions. The latest online systems reviewed in the next section have attempted to minimize those concerns. Faculty resistance regarding issues of *low response rates and negative bias* are examined in Flashpoint 6. The problem of *lack of standardized administration* is covered in Flashpoint 5, and certain types of *scale response bias* tend to be the same for both paper and online modes. Finally, the research related to the charge of *lower online ratings than paper-based ratings* is summarized in a subsequent section of this flashpoint.

Three Online Delivery Options

Online administration, scoring, analysis, and reporting of student ratings can be handled in three ways: (1) *in-house*, by the IT department or computer services center, center for teaching and learning, or an equivalent unit or combination of units; (2) *out-house*, by a vendor that provides all delivery and reporting services for the institution's "home-grown" scale; or (3) *out-house*, by a vendor that provides all services plus their own scale or a scale you create from their catalog of items. These options are listed in order of increasing cost. Depending on in-house resources, it is possible to execute the entire processing in a very cost-effective manner. Alternatively, estimates from a variety of vendors should be obtained for the out-house options.

In-House Administration

If you have developed or plan to develop your own scale, you should consider this option. The whole student-rating-scale operation should be housed in the IT or computer services center (CSC), center for teaching and learning (CTL), testing and assessment center (TAC), office of institutional research (OIR), or another creatively named unit with a three-letter acronym or a combination of units. There are specific advantages and disadvantages to various combinations, especially CSC and CTL. It is crucial that the "house of scaling" be independent of all faculty, except those faculty serving initially on the development committee. Once the scale(s) is finalized, they should NOT have access to any forms or data, unless authorized by the FBI, CIA, or NCIS. See how important these acronyms are? This policy is to assure complete confidentiality throughout the process for students and all personnel involved.

Convene the key players who can make this student-rating-scale adventure a reality, including administrators and staff from IT or CSC, CTL, and TAC, plus at least one measurement expert (in-house or out-house consultant). *A discussion of scale design, scoring, analysis, report design, and distribution can initially determine whether the resources are available to execute the system.* Once a preliminary assessment of the space, IT, and human resources required has been completed, costs should be estimated for each phase. A couple of meetings can provide enough information to consider the possibility.

Your in-house-system components, products, and personnel can then be compared to the two options described next. As you go shopping for an online system, at least *you will have done your homework* and be able to identify what the commercial vendors are offering, including qualitative differences, that you can't execute yourself. Although the commercial cost could be a deal-breaker, you will know all the options available to make an informed final decision. Further, you can always change your system if your stocks plummet, the in-house operation has too many bumps that can't be squished and ends up in Neverland, or the commercial services do not deliver as promised.

Vendor Administration With "Home-Grown" Scale

If outsourcing to a vendor is your preference, or you just want to explore this option but you want to *maintain control over your own scale content and structure*, there are certain vendors that can online your scale. For some strange reason, they're all located in Madagascar. Kidding. They include CollegeNET (*What Do You Think?*), ConnectEDU (*CoursEval*), Evaluation-KIT (*Online Course Evaluation and Survey System*), and IOTA Solutions (*MyClassEvaluation*). They will *administer your scale online, perform all analyses, and generate reports for different decision makers*. Thoroughly compare all of their components with yours. Evaluate the pluses and minuses of each package.

Make sure to investigate the *compatibility of the packages with your course management system*. The choice of the system is crucial to providing anonymity for students, which can boost response rates (Oliver & Sautter, 2005). Most of the vendors' packages are compatible with *Blackboard, WebCT, Moodle, Sakai*, and other campus portal systems.

There are even *free online survey providers*, such as *Zoomerang* (Market-Tools, 2006), which can be *used easily by any instructor without a course management system* (Hong, 2008). Other online survey software, both free and pay, has been reviewed by Wright (2005). There are specific advantages and disadvantages of the different packages, especially in regard to rating scale structure and reporting score results (Hong, 2008). This is a *viable online option* worth investigating for *formative feedback*.

Vendor Administration and Rating Scale

If you want a vendor to supply the rating scale and all the delivery services, there are several commercial student rating systems you should consider. Examples include *Online Course Evaluation, Student Instructional Report II*

(*SIR II*), *Course/Instructor Evaluation Questionnaire* (*CIEQ*), *IDEA Student Ratings of Instruction, Students' Evaluations of Educational Quality* (*SEEQ*), *Instructional Assessment System* (*IAS Online*), and *Purdue Instructor Course Evaluation Service* (*PICES*).

Here is *the simplest solution to an online student-rating-scale system:* Just go buy one. The seven packages are designed for you, Professor Consumer. The items are professionally developed; the scale has usually undergone extensive psychometric analyses to provide evidence of reliability and validity; and there are a variety of services provided, including the scale, online administration, scanning, scoring, and reporting of results in a variety of formats with national norms. With some, you can access a specimen set of rating scales and report forms online. All the vendors provide a list of services and prices on their websites.

Carefully shop around to *find the best fit for your faculty and administrator needs and institutional culture.* The packages vary considerably in scale design, administration options, report forms, norms, and, of course, cost. Any of the packages might work, as long as six criteria are satisfied (Berk, 2006):

> *Criterion 1.* The rating scale measures the job domain specifications of instructor behaviors and course characteristics in your institution.
>
> *Criterion 2.* The scale, online administration and processing, and report forms are appropriate for your faculty and the decisions to be made with ratings.
>
> *Criterion 3.* The scale satisfies standards for technical quality.
>
> *Criterion 4.* Your faculty buys in to the products and procedures developed by the vendor.
>
> *Criterion 5.* Online administration and reporting are compatible with your institution's course management system.
>
> *Criterion 6.* You get a financial windfall to subsidize this system from a relative you've never heard of in Nigeria who would like to transfer five hundred bazillion dollars to your bank for a small fee.

Criteria 2 and 4 are absolutely essential. Because your faculty members will be held accountable for the results of whatever rating scale is used, they should have input into the choice of that scale. They are the primary stakeholders. The items must be fair and appropriate for the f2f (face-to-face), blended/hybrid, and online courses and teaching methods in your departments. At minimum, a comprehensive critique of the selected scale should be conducted along with a thorough review of all other components in the package.

Comparability of Paper-and-Pencil and Online Ratings

Numerous studies have compared student ratings on structured items and their technical properties between paper-and-pencil and online administrations of scales, as well as ratings on unstructured items between both types of administration. Here are the results.

Structured Items

Despite all the differences between paper-based and online administrations and the contaminating response biases that afflict the ratings they produce, researchers consistently have found that on structured items *online students and their in-class counterparts rate courses and instructors similarly* (Avery, Bryan, Mathios, Kang, & Bell, 2006; Benton, Webster, Gross, & Pallett, 2010b; Carini, Hayek, Kuh, & Ouimet, 2003; Dommeyer, Baum, Hanna, & Chapman, 2004; Hardy, 2003; Layne, DeCristoforo, & McGinty, 1999; McGhee & Lowell, 2003; Perrett, 2011; Spooner, Jordan, Algozzine, & Spooner, 1999; Stowell, Addison, & Smith, 2012; Venette, Sellnow, & McIntire, 2010; Waschull, 2001). That is, the ratings on the structured items are not systematically higher or lower for online administrations. The correlations between online and paper-based global item ratings were .84 (overall instructor) and .86 (overall course) (Johnson, 2003).

Although the ratings for online and paper are not identical, with more than 70% of the variance in common, any differences in ratings that have been found are small. Further, *interrater reliability of ratings on individual items and item clusters for both modalities have been found to be comparable* (McGhee & Lowell, 2003), *and so have the underlying factor structures* (Layne et al., 1999; Leung & Kember, 2005). All these similarities were also found when f2f and online courses were compared; however, response rates were slightly lower in the online courses (Benton, Webster, Gross, & Pallett, 2010a).

Alpha total scale (18-item) reliabilities were similar for paper-based (.90) and online (.88) modes when all items appeared on the screen (Peer & Gamliel, 2011). Slightly lower coefficients (.74.–83) for online displays of one, two, or four items only on the screen were attributable to response bias (Berk, 2010; Gamliel & Davidovitz, 2005; Peer & Gamliel, 2011).

Unstructured Items

The one exception to the similarities in results from online and paper-based administration is in the unstructured items, or open-ended comment section. The research has indicated that the flexible time permitted to the online responders usually, but not always, yields *longer and more frequent and thoughtful comments than those of in-class respondents* (Anderson et al., 2005; Burton, Civitano, & Steiner-Grossman, 2012; Donovan, Mader, & Shinsky, 2006; Hardy, 2002, 2003; Johnson, 2001, 2003; Layne et al., 1999; Morrison, 2011; Ravelli, 2000; Venette et al., 2010). Students report that typing the responses is easier and faster than writing them, plus it *preserves their anonymity* (Johnson, 2003; Layne et al., 1999).

Recommendations

The results of weighing all the pluses and minuses in this section strongly suggest that *the conversion from a paper-based to online system of administering student rating scales is worthy of serious consideration by every institution of higher education.* When the concerns about the online approach are investigated, its benefits for f2f, blended/hybrid, and online/distance courses have been found to far outweigh the benefits of the traditional paper-based approach. (*NOTE:* Online administration should also be employed for alumni ratings and employer ratings. The costs for these ratings will be a small fraction of the cost of the student rating system.)

7

FLASHPOINT 5

Standardized vs. Unstandardized Online Scale Administration

Standardized administration procedures for any measure of human or rodent behavior are absolutely essential to be able to interpret the ratings with the same meaning for all individuals who completed the measure. Student rating scales are typically administered online at the end of the semester without regard for any standardization or controls. There don't seem to be any sound psychometric reasons for why scale administrations are scheduled the way they are. This is, perhaps, the most neglected issue in the literature and in practice.

Importance of Standardization

Asignificant amount of attention has been devoted to establishing standardized times, conditions, locations, and procedures for administering in-class tests and clinical measures, such as the objective structured clinical examination (OSCE), as well as out-of-class admissions, licensing, and certification tests. National standards for testing practices require this standardization *to assure that students take tests under identical conditions* so their scores (a) can be interpreted in the same way, (b) are comparable from one student or group to another, and (c) can be compared to norms (AERA, APA, & NCME Joint Committee on Standards, 1999).

45

What's the Problem?

The problem is that deliberate steps are rarely taken to assure standardization of all online administration procedures. This section examines (a) current practices; (b) confounding, uncontrolled factors; and (c) timing of administration.

Current Practices

Unfortunately, *standardization has been completely neglected in the faculty evaluation literature for the administration of online student rating scales* (Berk, 2006). Although the inferences that will be drawn from the scale ratings and other measures of teaching effectiveness require holding to the same administration precision as for tests, procedures to assure ratings will have the same meaning from all students completing the scales at the end of the semester have not been addressed in research and practice. Typically, *students are given notice that they have one or two weeks to complete the online student ratings form, and the deadline is before or after the final exam or project.* This practice precludes any standardization of the administration.

Confounding, Uncontrolled Factors

Because students can complete online rating scales outside the classroom during their discretionary time, *the institution has no control over the time, place, conditions, or any situational factors* under which the self-administrations occur (Addison & Stowell, 2012; Stowell et al., 2012). Most of these factors were controlled in paper-and-pencil, in-class administration by the professor or a student appointed to handle the administration.

In fact, in the online mode, *there is no way to ensure that the real student filled out the form or didn't discuss it with someone who already did.* It could be a roommate, partner, avatar, alien, a student who has never been to class doing a favor in exchange for a pizza, brewskies, or an iPhone, or all of the preceding. Any of those substitutes would result in *fraudulent ratings* (Standard 5.6). Bad, bad ratings!

Timing of Administration

One of the biggest uncontrolled factors is the timing of the administration, which can markedly affect the ratings. For example, when a student completes the scale before the final review and final exam, on the day of the final, or after the exam, his or her feelings about the instructor or course can be very different. *Exposure to the final exam alone can significantly affect ratings,* particularly if there are specific items on the scale measuring testing and evaluation methods. It could be argued that the final should be completed in order to provide a true rating of all evaluation methods.

Despite a couple of "no significant difference" studies of paper-and-pencil administrations almost 40 years ago (Carrier, Howard, & Miller, 1974; Frey, 1976) and one study examining final-exam-day administration (Ory, 2001) that produced lower ratings, *there doesn't seem to be any agreement among the experts on the best time to administer online scales or on any specific standardization procedures* other than standardized directions.

What is clear is that whatever timing is decided on must be the same for all students in all courses; otherwise, the ratings of these different groups of students will not have the same meaning. For example, *faculty within a department should agree that all online administrations must be completed before the final exam or after, but not both.* Faculty must decide on the best time to get the most accurate ratings. That decision will also affect the legitimacy of any comparison of the ratings to different norm groups.

Standards for Standardization

So what's wrong with the lack of standardization? The ratings by students are *assumed* to be collected under identical conditions according to the same rules and directions. Scales administered following standardized procedures in a standardized environment provide a snapshot of how students feel at one point in time. Although their individual ratings will vary, they will have the same meaning. Rigorous procedures for standardization are required by the *Standards for Educational and Psychological Testing* (AERA, APA, & NCME Joint Committee on Standards, 1999).

Groups of students must be given identical directions, which is possible, follow those directions, which is possible, and administered the scale under identical conditions, which is nearly impossible, to assure the comparability of their ratings (Standards 3.15, 3.19, and 3.20). Only then will the interpretation of the ratings and, in this case, the inferences about teaching effectiveness from the ratings be valid and reliable (Standard 3.19). In other words, *without standardization*—as when every student fills out the scale willy-nilly at different times of the day and semester, in different places, under different conditions, using different procedures—*the ratings from student to student and professor to professor will not be comparable.*

Recommendations

Given the limitations of online administration, what can be done to *approximate some semblance of standardized conditions* or, at least, to *minimize the extent to which the bad conditions contaminate the ratings?* Here are a few options extended from Berk's (2006) previous suggestions, presented from highest level of standardization and control to lowest level.

In-Class Administration Before Final Exam

This option provides *maximum control by setting a certain time slot in class,* just like the paper-and-pencil version, for students to complete the forms on their own PC/Mac, iPad, iPhone, iPencil, or other device. The professor should appoint a student to execute and monitor the process and leave the room to grab a snack with a low glycemic index or else a donut. Adequate time should be given for all students to type comments for the unstructured section of the scale. This option also will yield a very high response rate (see Flashpoint 6, Strategy 20). (*NOTE:* This option is not recommended if there are several items or a subscale that measures course evaluation methods because it occurs before the final, which is part of those methods.)

Computer Lab Time Slots Before or After Final

Set certain time slots in the computer lab or an equivalent location during which students can complete the forms. The controls exercised in the previous option should be followed in the lab. Techie-type students should proctor the slots to eliminate distractions and provide technical support for any problems that arise. This option also can significantly increase the students' response rate (see Flashpoint 6, Strategy 20).

One or Two Days Before or After Final at Students' Discretion

This is *the most loosy-goosy option,* albeit the most popular, *with the least control.* Specify a *narrow window* (preferably Andersen® or Pella®) within which the ratings must be completed, such as *one or two days after the final class and before the final exam* OR *one or two days after the exam and before grades are submitted and posted.* This can be a "storm window."

Conclusion

Any one of the preceding three options will improve the standardization of current online administration practices beyond the typical one- or two-week bay window. Hopefully, experience and research on these procedures will identify the confounding variables that can affect the online ratings and test strategies in order to minimize or eliminate them. Eventually, this should result in concrete guidelines to assist faculty in deciding on the most appropriate administration protocol.

8

FLASHPOINT 6

Low Online-Administration Response Rates

Since online administrations of student rating scales began over a decade ago, response rates have been consistently lower than for their paper-and-pencil predecessor, where the professor controlled the in-class response rate with a student administrator and collector. In some cases, online response rates have been 50% and even lower, which pretty much render the ratings useless for decision making. Faculty members at various institutions have used that excuse to resist the online conversion. Research and experience with the online administration process have produced more than 20 different strategies to increase response rates, which have crept back up to percentages in the 70s and even 90s at some colleges.

What's the Problem?

The problem with low response rates on a student rating scale is that they *provide an inadequate data base from which to infer teaching effectiveness* from the ratings as well as other measures. If the percentage of responses is too small, the sampling error can be frightfully large, and the representativeness of the students who did respond can be biased. The nonresponse bias also becomes a concern. These biases significantly diminish the usefulness of the ratings and make administrators very unhappy.

What Are the Reasons?

The research on this topic indicates the following possible reasons students don't respond: *apathy, technical problems, perceived lack of anonymity, lack of importance, inconvenience, inaccessibility, time for completion, social texting, and how it cuts into party time at the end of the semester* (Adams & Umbach, 2012; Avery et al., 2006; Ballantyne, 2002, 2003; Dommeyer, Baum, & Hanna, 2002; Sorenson & Reiner, 2003). Recent improvements in the design and execution of online delivery systems have, at least, reduced and, in some cases, eliminated most of those perceptions.

Faculty members also have had concerns that dissatisfied students are more likely to respond than other students (Johnson, 2003). This possible *negative response bias* was not supported by Kherfi (2011) and Benton et al.'s (2010b) study that found low correlations between response rate and student ratings.

Determinants of Criterion Response Rate

Statistical Guidelines

Although the minimum response rate based on sampling error for a seminar with 10 students may be different from a class of 50, 100, or larger, rates in the 80% to 100% range will be adequate for most any class size. Statistical tables of response rates for different errors and confidence intervals are available (Nulty, 2008).

Unfortunately, the *rules of survey sampling do not provide a simple statistical answer* to the response rate question for online rating scales. The class size that responds (sample) in relation to the total class size (population) is not the only issue. There are at least two major sources of error to consider: (1) *standard error of the mean rating* based on sample size and (2) *standard error of measurement* based on the reliability of the item, subscale, or total scale ratings. Confidence intervals can be computed for both.

In typical survey research, inferences about characteristics of the population are drawn from the sample statistics. Only *decisions about groups* are rendered; not about individuals. In contrast, the inferences from sample (class) ratings are used for teaching improvement (formative) and important career (summative) *decisions about individual professors. The response rate for one type of decision may not be adequate for other types of decisions.* There are several nonstatistical factors that should be considered.

Nonstatistical Factors

There are at least three factors that qualify the acceptable or tolerable response rate:

1. *Importance of decision.* Using ratings to change the order of topics in a course syllabus is not the same as using them to decide on contract renewal of an instructor. Formative decisions use anchor and item statistics to flag areas for possible teaching and course changes; summative decisions based on total and subscale ratings across courses over a year or longer can affect a faculty member's career (see Flashpoint 9). The latter requires a higher level of precision, as measured by standard errors, because of its greater importance than the former.

2. *Availability of corroborative information.* When ratings on one scale are biased due to low response rate, the decision maker can consider ratings from other scales or data that can provide corroborative information. For example, unstructured "comments" from students, especially from a scale administered online, can confirm, explain, or disconfirm the item means/medians from the structured ratings. Although such comments arguably may not be the best alternative, they provide a credible default when the structured ratings are questionable for suggesting course changes.

3. *Availability of other sources of evidence.* Ratings from other sources that may not be corroborative, but which are valuable for triangulating because of the information they provide on teaching effectiveness, can be weighted more heavily in decisions than ratings that were discredited because of low response rate. Peer ratings of teaching and course materials may serve as useful alternative sources.

Minimum Acceptable Rate

When response rate is contextualized (*NOTE TO SELF:* Insert hilarious joke here.) in terms of the decisions to be made and the availability of other evidence, the statistical estimates based on the standard errors mentioned previously need to be adjusted. Considering all these factors, here are some rules of thumb for acceptable response rates. In other words, this is what you've been waiting for all chapter long:

- *Formative decisions with or without other data:* At least 60% may be tolerable to direct teaching and course modifications.

Worst Case Scenario: If the changes are misdirected or don't work based on subsequent feedback or data, corrections can be made easily; that is, *wrong decisions from biased, evil ratings are not irrevocable.*

* *Summative decisions:* At least 80% per course would be required when ratings are used alone, but 70% when two or more other sources are considered. For these decisions, a higher level of precision is required. *Worst Case Scenario:* If personnel decisions based on these response rates or lower are incorrect, such as nonrenewal of an annual contract, *they cannot be easily corrected or reversed.* Only if new, compelling information should surface to the contrary would consideration be given to overturning these decisions. The stakes are much higher for all summative decisions.

Current Response Rates

How do the preceding guidelines match up against current response rates? Not well! The percentages of responses to online administrations have been reported in the *50s*, in contrast to the 70s and 80s of paper-based administration (Benton et al., 2010b). The preceding "rules" require the latter range or higher. Unfortunately, the *online rates have been consistently lower than paper* at several institutions (Anderson et al., 2005; Avery et al., 2006; Mau & Opengart, 2012; Morrison, 2011; Nowell, Gale, & Handley, 2010; Nulty, 2008; Sax, Gilmartin, & Bryant, 2003; Sid Nair, Adams, & Mertova, 2008; Stowell et al., 2012). This is a frequent objection to online ratings reported in faculty surveys (Crews & Curtis, 2011). Fear of low response rates has been one of the major deterrents to some institutions' adopting online systems. So what can be done to improve these rates?

Top 20 Strategies to Boost Response Rates

Survey researchers have examined the *use of a variety of incentives* (Toepoel, 2012) in online surveys (Bennett & Sid Nair, 2010; Van Selm & Jankowski, 2006), including vouchers and lottery prizes (Deutskens, de Ruyter, Wetzels, & Oosterveld, 2004; Gajic, Cameron, & Hurley, 2011; Laguilles, Williams, & Saunders, 2011), as pre- and post-incentives (Sánchez-Fernández, Muñoz-Leiva, Montoro-Ríos, & Ibáñez-Zapata, 2010), compared to disincentives and no incentives. Guess what? *Vouchers and a lottery with a small number of large prizes or small prizes with a higher chance of winning generate the highest response rates to surveys.* Although these and other incentives can contribute to raising rates in surveys, they have not been studied with online student rating scales.

Administrators, faculty, and students at several institutions have tested a variety of strategies to increase response rates to online administrations of student rating scales. Here is the BERKO COLLECTION™ (available at Walmart®) of *20 of the most effective strategies* (Adams, 2012; Adams & Umbach, 2012; Berk, 2006, in press; Dommeyer et al., 2004; IDEA Center, 2008; Johnson, 2003; Sorenson & Reiner, 2003). They are grouped according to the person responsible for executing the strategy—the coordinator or director of the online system *and* faculty and administrators.

Coordinator/Director of Online System

1. Manages online system; coordinates among the department, center for teaching and learning or assessment (see Flashpoint 4), and/or vendor; and monitors the entire process, independent of faculty (Berk, 2006)
2. Specifies purpose(s) of ratings (e.g., teaching improvement, salary, promotion, tenure) in the scale's directions (Benton & Cashin, 2012; Berk, 2006) to provide accountability in the process, despite a couple of studies indicating such specification has minimal effects on ratings (Centra, 1976; Marsh, 2007)
3. Assures ease of computer access and navigation on campus (Sorenson & Reiner, 2003)
4. Monitors use of technology (PCs/Macs, iPads, etc.) and procedures for in-class or online administration (IDEA Center, 2008)
5. Assures anonymity and confidentiality (Adams, 2012; Berk, 2006; IDEA Center, 2008; Sorenson & Reiner, 2003)
6. Provides simple, explicit instructions on how to use the system (Dommeyer et al., 2004; Johnson, 2003; Norris & Conn, 2005)
7. Maintains a convenient, user-friendly system (Layne et al., 1999; Ravelli, 2000; Sid Nair & Adams, 2009; Sorenson & Reiner, 2003)
8. Sends reminders to all students before the window of response opens, then frequent reminders during window only to students who have not responded (Adams, 2012; Cook, Heath, & Thompson, 2000; Dommeyer et al., 2004; Sid Nair et al., 2008)
9. Plans ad campaigns to inform students of the rating scale process, online and in student publications (IDEA Center, 2008)

10. Provides school-wide incentives, such as a lottery for an iPad, iPhone, or some other iGadget, bookstore items, or food coupons (Ballantyne, 2003; Johnson, 2003)

11. Acknowledges and rewards faculty and/or departments that meet the target response rate (IDEA Center, 2008) (*NOTE:* Make sure this "healthy competition" doesn't affect the integrity of the process.)

12. Promotes donor/alumni contributions of a specified dollar amount to a charity for every form completed (Ravenscroft & Enyeart, 2009)

13. Communicates the notion that evaluation of teaching and the students' formal feedback in that process are part of the campus culture and their responsibility (IDEA Center, 2008)

14. Permits students early access to final course grades ASAP after the end of the course (Anderson, Brown, & Spaeth, 2006; Berk, 2006; Dommeyer et al., 2004; Johnson, 2003)

Faculty and Administrators

15. Deans, department chairs, and faculty communicate to students the importance of their input (Berk, 2006; Johnson, 2003; Sorenson & Reiner, 2003)

16. Faculty emphasize the intended purpose(s) of the ratings (IDEA Center, 2008)

17. Faculty strongly encourage and remind students to complete forms (Adams, 2012; IDEA Center, 2008)

18. Faculty "assign" students to complete forms as part of their course grade (Ravenscroft & Enyeart, 2009)

19. Faculty provide positive incentives, such as extra credit or points, dropping a low grade on an assignment or quiz (Dommeyer et al., 2004; Johnson, 2003; Prunty, 2011), movie or restaurant vouchers, cruise tickets, or vacation packages to Rio

20. Faculty set an in-class time to simulate the "captive audience" concept of the paper-and-pencil administration, but this time with laptops, iPads, iPods, or iPhones to complete forms; also computer lab or chat-room times can be reserved for this purpose (IDEA Center, 2008; see Flashpoint 5 "Recommendations" for details)

Recommendations

As you process the preceding list, there will be several strategies that will strike your fancy (cruise and trip to Rio) and fit into your online system.

However, there are others that may incite you to riot because you perceive them as unethical (e.g., "assigning" the scale or dropping a low grade), somewhat questionable (e.g., vouchers and lotteries), or even illegal (e.g., bribes and early access to grades). At least, there are lots of options.

Which ones should you pick? The next section proffers six guidelines.

Combinations of Strategies

Reports by the researchers, administrators, and undercover police officers who have tested these various strategies indicate

- Administrative and organizational procedures 1 through 8 are essential.
- Incentives 9 through 13 are variable in terms of increased response rate.
- Early posting of grades via 14 has produced the highest increase of any single strategy.
- Administrative procedures 15 through 17 are highly recommended.
- Incentives 18 and 19 are the most contentious.
- Administration option 20 can produce response rates comparable to paper-based version.

Pick the "Right" Combination

Overall, it is the right combination of administrative procedures and incentives that can yield response percentages in the 70s through 90s. The administrator of the online system and faculty must decide on the *magical combination that will receive the commitment of all stakeholders* involved in the process and be compatible with the campus culture. The system must then be executed properly to assure a high RSOI (rate of student return on the online investment) or other lame acronym.

Future Response Rates

Once the system is implemented, your job isn't over. I bet you were packing your bags for Rio. Too bad. Instead, *think about how the students will remember their "rating experience."* This applies to all courses—f2f, online, and blended/hybrid. If the experience was positive and meaningful, then they'll probably participate the next semester; if it was negative because of administrative or technical glitches, was too time-consuming, was perceived as a waste of time, or infringed on party activities, then expect response rates to tank. The design and operation of the online administration will be key determinants of whether students will continue to complete the forms.

Students' expectations about how the results will be used are also critical to future response rates. Chen and Hoshower (2003) found that *students' motivation to participate* in the rating system again hinged on the following semi-observable outcomes (in order of decreasing importance): (1) improvements in teaching, (2) improvements in course content and format, and (3) faculty personnel decisions (promotion, tenure, salary increase).

Closing the Loop

Changes. The efforts to make changes and the actual changes that occur based on the results are often referred to as "closing the ~~deal~~ loop" (Bennett & Sid Nair, 2010) or "loop de loop." I forget which. It builds credibility and administrative accountability into the system. The changes convey: "~~We don't mess around; we mean business.~~" "Student ratings are meaningful and important." Students' input or feedback really matters. They are engaged as active participants in the process of evaluating teaching effectiveness.

No changes. Students' iBalls and iPhones will be riveted on the follow-up actions taken by your administrators and faculty. Their texting grapevine is extremely effective. Contrary to the preceding scenario, suppose students do not see any results. Their expectations are explicit because the intended purposes of the ratings were stated in the directions on the scale. Those words need to be backed up with observable changes. If not, why should they bother to complete the forms the next time they're asked? If those purposes are not fulfilled, the response rates can nosedive.

Conclusion

Overall, the *students' role in completing the rating scales online is an essential antecedent to the success of the evaluation system.* However, looping is required: All of these elements described in this section are interconnected and must work together effectively to assure seamless execution of the online system and high response rates from year to year.

9

FLASHPOINT 7
Global Items vs. Total Scale Rating

One of the simplest indicators of teaching or course effectiveness is student ratings on one or more global items from the entire rating scale. This has been recommended by a few researchers to get a quick-read, at-a-glance summary for summative decisions. It is used in lieu of the total scale rating or the subscale ratings. The issue is the choice between making a decision, such as contract renewal or a pay raise, based on one or two global items or on the single rating based on all the scale items. How much information is needed for summative decisions? What is the difference in the reliability and validity of these single rating options?

Definition of a *Global Item*

"What in the world is a *global item*?" Here are a few examples that can be rated with a "Strongly Disagree" to "Strongly Agree" anchor scale:

- Overall, this instructor was an excellent teacher.
- Overall, this course was excellent.
- Overall, my instructor is a dirt bag.
- Overall, this course is putrid.
- Overall, I learned squat in this course.

This type of item provides a general *broad-stroke, summary index of teaching performance or course quality*. It doesn't address specific teaching and course characteristics. Global items typically appear at the end of the student rating scale so students have had time to form an opinion after responding to all the items. They should not be summed with the ratings of all other items; they are reported separately, independent of the rest of the scale.

Use for Summative Decisions

In the 1990s administrators, such as department chairs, directors, and associate deans, were encouraged to use the ratings on global items to provide a *simple, quick-and-easy measure of teaching effectiveness for summative decisions* (Abrami & d'Apollonia, 1991; Algozzine et al., 2004; Braskamp & Ory, 1994; Cashin & Downey, 1992; Cashin et al., 1994; Centra, 1993; d'Apollonia & Abrami, 1997a; Hativa & Raviv, 1993). More recently, administrators expressed a preference for the use of global items for information on the overall quality of the course and instructor (Beran, Violato, & Kline, 2007; Beran, Violato, Kline, & Frideres, 2005).

What's the Problem?

Despite the simplicity and ease with which an administrator can use a single global item rating for summative decisions about faculty, that use is *inappropriate for personnel decisions about employees*. There are several sets of standards that specify the types of ratings that are required for such decisions. The global item does not satisfy all those standards. The next section explains why.

Critical Standards

Given the seriousness of decisions on a professor's condition of employment and career, *critical standards should be met by all administrators* who are responsible (Berk, 2013b). The standards can be sorted into four categories: (1) psychometric, (2) representativeness and fairness, (3) professional, and (4) legal.

Psychometric Standards

Item validity evidence.   Cashin and Downey (1992) studied two global items:

- "Overall, I rate this INSTRUCTOR an excellent teacher," and
- "Overall, I rate this COURSE as excellent."

They found that these items accounted for more than 50% of the variance in a composite criterion measure—the *Instructional Development and Effectiveness Assessment* (*IDEA*). When this study was replicated with four other criteria using *IDEA* data (Cashin et al., 1994), the result was the same: *a body of validity evidence showing that the global items accounted for most of the variance in several criterion measures of teaching effectiveness.* This prompted the researchers to recommend the use of those items for summative decisions.

Although global item-total scale and subscale correlations are rarely reported, there is also evidence that those combinations are highly intercorrelated (Harrison, Douglas, & Burdsall, 2004; Hativa & Raviv, 1993; Otani, Kim, & Cho, 2012; Wanous & Hudy, 2001). Item intercorrelations among course and instructor global items and items on teaching methods and student progress on course outcomes were consistently moderate to high for the *IDEA Student Ratings of Instruction* form (Benton et al., 2010b).

So, with all this compelling validity evidence, *why not substitute the global rating for the total scale rating?* Wouldn't that be a reasonable proxy? Not exactly. Don't forget about the other type of evidence, validity's closest pal—*reliability*, which leads us nicely into the next paragraph.

Item reliability evidence. The issue is what's NOT usually computed: the reliability of the global item rating. Rarely are global item reliabilities estimated for student rating scales. When they are, they can be lower than necessary for individual decision making. They should be in the mid .80s to .90s.

[*FOR RESEARCHERS ONLY:* Typically, *item reliabilities computed from class means can be in the .70s to .90s* (Ginns & Barrie, 2004; Lucas & Donnellan, 2012; Wanous & Hudy, 2001) *for unidimensional scales*, depending on the method used to estimate them (test-retest, intraclass correlation, correction for attenuation, or factor analysis). That range of coefficients can be illustrated with the Spearman rho split-half coefficients of .75 to .91 (class sizes = 10 to 34) and the .90s (class sizes = 35 and above) for the global items on the *IDEA Student Ratings of Instruction* form (Hoyt & Lee, 2002).]

The problem is that *coefficients in the .70s are too low and unstable for single global items to be used for decisions about individual employees.* Because those items are usually found on multidimensional scales, the item reliabilities can be even lower. Such coefficients have been found for different healthcare single-item measures of stress (Littman, White, Satia, Bowen, & Kristal, 2006), physical functioning and emotional health (DeSalvo, Fisher,

Tran, Bloser, Merrill, & Peabody, 2006), and quality of life (Yohannes, Dodd, Morris, & Webb, 2011). In contrast to these low reliabilities, the *reliability coefficients in the mid .80s to .90s* published in the student ratings literature are usually *for the total or subscale collections of items.*

Item versus total scale rating reliability.   Despite the strong validity evidence underpinning global items, the previous differences in reliabilities raise a serious technical concern about the utility of global items, inasmuch as their ratings are used for summative personnel decisions about faculty. *Their potential for unacceptably low coefficients renders them inappropriate for any decisions about individual faculty members.* The strongest psychometric evidence rests with total and subscale ratings; the least stable is associated with the global items. Consider what foundation should be used to make decisions, for example, about contract renewal: one or two global items or the total scale rating based on 15 to 35 items.

Representativeness and Fairness

Item representativeness.   After students have spent 45 hours, or a time close to that, in a course over the semester, suppose they rate the global item "Overall, I rate this instructor as an excellent teacher," as part of a total scale. *Does the rating on that item seem to accurately capture the sum total of all the teaching behaviors those students observed in their f2f or online course?* The percentages of explained variance in the research mentioned previously indicate it comes close. Can it represent that domain of behaviors? Will it reflect the differences between an f2f and online course?

There is no doubt that the global item furnishes information about teaching effectiveness based on the validity studies, but should it be used for summative, super-important decisions about a professor's career? *Is one item rating of 0 to 3 or 4 an adequate, reasonable base from which teaching effectiveness can be inferred?* How fair is that? As Edward Nuhfer (2010) argued, the evaluation of teaching, as a fractal form with complicated neural networks, is far too complex to be reduced to a single item. (*NOTE:* I have no clue what that means, but I wanted to acknowledge Ed "Fractal" Nuhfer's work, which supported my argument, kinda.)

Performance appraisal ratings.   Hypothetically, could you accurately and fairly rate the performance of your administrative assistant, department chair, or dean with one item to truly measure his or her performance or degree of effectiveness? Would he or she want you to do that?

For more than half a century, *performance appraisals of employees in business and industry* typically have involved scale ratings by several professionals who are in the best positions to evaluate their performance (Bracken, Timmreck, & Church, 2001; Edwards & Ewen, 1996; Lepsinger & Lucia, 2009). These appraisals are significant because of the importance of decisions regarding employment and, therefore, of feedback given to employees to improve their performance.

This evidence of job performance is *not only based on the ratings of all relevant job behaviors, but is also by multiple qualified raters.* No single item can furnish that type of information; however, there have been global item measures of job satisfaction (Dolbier, Webster, McCalister, Mallon, & Steinhardt, 2005; Wanous, Reichers, & Hudy, 1997). The way evaluations of teaching effectiveness are conducted can and should be similar to those performance appraisals with multiple ratings by different raters (Berk, 2009b).

Professional Standards for Employee Decisions

Standards for Educational and Psychological Testing.   Relying on one or two global ratings alone for major summative decisions about faculty performance is totally inadequate. That administrative practice *violates U.S. testing/ scaling standards* according to the *Standards for Educational and Psychological Testing* (AERA, APA, & NCME Joint Committee on Standards, 1999). Clearly, these are *personnel decisions* about employees, not program decisions related to instruction or the curriculum. In the case of employee decisions like these, *one or two items do not reflect an accurate assessment of the instructor's job behaviors* (Standard 14.8). A total scale rating based on, for example, 35 items matched to the domain of teaching behaviors, or subscale ratings on specific areas of teaching competency, would satisfy Standards 14.9 and 14.10 that require *a close link between the job content and the rating items.* Further, according to Standard 2.1, *reliability should be estimated for total, subscale, and combination ratings*, not for single items.

Personnel Evaluation Standards.   The preceding standards are also supported by the latest edition of the *Personnel Evaluation Standards* (Joint Committee on Educational Evaluation Standards, 2009). The use of global items would not be upheld by Standards A4 (Valid Measurement) and A5 (Reliable Measurement). These standards require, among other criteria, that the scale include a representative sample of job tasks, that inferences about the professor are drawn from the scale, and that the ratings provide consistent (i.e., reliable) measurements of the professor's performance. *A single item rating cannot satisfy any of those requirements.*

Legal Standards for Employee Decisions

Employment instrument EEOC Guidelines.   Because instruments can be used to hire, promote, demote, or fire an employee, the U.S. Equal Employment Opportunity Commission's (EEOC) *Uniform Guidelines on Employee Selection Procedures* (U.S. Code of Federal Regulations, 1978) set forth laws to protect an innocent employee from an evil employer who intentionally uses instruments to discriminate based on pay, age, color, disability, national origin, pregnancy, race, religion, or sex. Such uses violate *federal antidiscrimination laws involving "disparate impact"* (i.e., practices that result in a disproportionate "adverse impact" on members of a minority group) *and "disparate treatment"* (i.e., practices that result in "intentional" discrimination of certain people groups during the hiring, promoting, or placement process) (U.S. EEOC, 2010).

Employment tests and other procedures, like *rating scales of job performance*, must be (a) "job-related and consistent with business necessity," and (b) "properly validated for the positions and purposes for which they are used" (U.S. EEOC, 2010). They cannot be designed, intended, or used to discriminate. Further, *employers are not permitted to adjust the scores, use different cutoff scores* (see Flashpoint 9 on criterion-referenced rating interpretation), *or alter the results so as to discriminate against a particular group.* The complexity of this application of employment instruments and the "validation" requirements would *preclude global items from being used for any employment decisions about faculty.*

Employment instrument court cases.   A long history of court cases on employment testing practices indicates that *the instrument used to measure employee performance must be based on a comprehensive analysis of the job's tasks* related to a person's knowledge, skills, and abilities (KSAs) (Nathan & Cascio, 1986). In a review of 39 court of appeals cases and 43 district court cases from 2000 to 2007 (Ashe & U.S. EEOC, 2007), it was found that employment tests that produced "substantial adverse impact of a protected group" (see Flashpoint 9 for 80/20 rule) or "disparate impact" were scrutinized by the courts in terms of rigorous reliability and validity studies (Wines & Lau, 2006), especially in regard to *selected cutoff scores for the decisions that resulted in the "impact."* One or two global items wouldn't come close to satisfying that level of scrutiny.

Recommendations

Global items provide the illusion of (a) simplicity, (b) accurate and reliable information, and (c) the pinpoint precision needed for summative decisions about faculty. Unfortunately, *the single rating of a global item* can be *(a) unreliable, (b) unrepresentative of the domain of teaching behaviors it was intended to measure, and (c) inappropriate for personnel decisions according to U.S. professional and legal standards.* In fact, even if a global item were to satisfy the psychometric criteria, it would still fall short of meeting professional and legal standards for employment decisions. Further, Arreola (n.d.) found that global items are often misinterpreted and misunderstood as measures of faculty performance. This problem relates to the issue of "student ratings versus student evaluation" of those items (see Flashpoint Terminology, chapter 2).

"Cease and Desist" Use of Global Items

Although administrators have used global items for decisions about faculty teaching performance for quite some time and they are an attractive option, it is recommended that these practices come to a screeching halt. As noted previously, important, possibly career-changing *individual personnel decisions are held to the highest standards psychometrically, professionally, and legally,* as they should be. If you know an administrator who is engaging in such practices, he or she should be urged to "cease and desist" before he or she is ordered legally to do so.

Four Alternatives to Global Item Rating

So what's an administrator supposed to do? Here are a few options to consider:

1. Use the *total scale rating* (mean/median) as the summary index across all items for the professor's courses over the past year. They can be displayed as simple numbers or graphically (see Flashpoint 9 for examples).
2. Use *two composite ratings*: one based on all items measuring *instructor characteristics* and a second based on those items measuring *course*

characteristics. These two composites are far superior psychometrically to their global item counterparts and can also be presented for several courses.

3. Use *subscale (category) ratings* for different areas of teaching and course characteristics, which are consistent with the abundant evidence on the multidimensionality of student rating scales (see Flashpoint 9). Unfortunately, there is no agreement on the number of subscales based on the factors or dimensions that should be used for personnel decisions (Abrami & d'Apollonia, 1990; Apodaca & Grad, 2005; Harrison et al., 2004; Hativa & Raviv, 1993; Renaud & Murray, 2005). Those factors will vary with different scales.

The profile of subscale ratings furnishes information on the strengths and weaknesses of the instructor and course. When administrators view these category ratings over time and courses, they can identify areas of growth and progress or of "Peter Pan syndrome" (no growth). Some administrators may find that subscale ratings provide more information than they need, but at least all these ratings are available.

4. Use *any of the preceding options in conjunction with data from other measures* of teaching effectiveness, such as peer observations, self-ratings, teaching scholarship, administrator ratings, and teaching (course) portfolios.

Conclusion

These options would satisfy the *Standards for Educational and Psychological Testing* and *Personnel Evaluation Standards* cited previously. All the preceding options except option 4 draw on ratings readily available from the student rating scale. It is simply a matter of how the ratings are reported for individual courses and across courses for each faculty member. Option 4 requires information from other sources, which is preferable to using student ratings alone. Consider these options when reviewing report forms offered by vendors for online administration (see Flashpoint 4).

10

FLASHPOINT 8

Scoring "Neutral," "Not Applicable," "Not Observed," and Blank Answers

When students, peers, administrators, employers, extraterrestrials, and others answer an item on a rating scale, occasionally they don't pick one of the valid rating anchors; instead, they select an opt-out *or* escape *response, which may be the "Neutral (N)," "Not Applicable (NA)," or "Not Observed (NO)" option, or simply leave the item blank. Those responses give us no information on the respondent's opinion about the behavior being rated. More important, how do those responses affect the scoring of the scale? Do you score the responses with a secret formula to make the total rating the same as those who don't pick an opt-out response? This is troublesome. How do you handle those responses?*

"Neutral," "Uncertain," or "Undecided" Response

Bipolar scales, such as "Strongly Agree–Strongly Disagree" and "Satisfied–Dissatisfied," may have a midpoint option (on an odd-numbered scale with five or seven points, for example) that serves as an escape anchor. When a respondent picks this anchor, he or she is usually thinking:

- "I have no opinion, belief, or attitude on this statement."
- "I'm too lazy to take a position on this right now."

- "I don't care because I need to do my laundry or I'll be going to class naked."

The respondent is essentially refusing to commit to a position for whatever reason. From a measurement perspective, the information provided on teaching performance from a neutral response is NOTHING! ZIPPO! NADA! QUE PASA! *By not forcing students to take a position by either agreeing or disagreeing with the item, information is lost forever.* How sad. Further, when several students pick the midpoint for an item and the overall ratings are generally favorable (aka negatively skewed), the faculty rating on the item can be lower or more conservative than when respondents are forced to commit to a position.

For rating scales used to measure teaching effectiveness, *it is recommended that the midpoint position be omitted* and an even-numbered scale be used, such as four or six points. If the items are correctly written and all students, peers, and administrators are in a position to render an informed opinion on the professor's behavior, then all items should be answered.

"Not Applicable" (NA) Response

"Not Applicable" means *the respondent cannot answer because the statement is ~~dumb~~ irrelevant* or doesn't apply to the person or object being rated. Having a few items on a rating scale that might be interpreted as not applicable or inappropriate by some students can be not only irritating and confusing but also misleading. It can make students angry, violent, or stop responding to the items.

Where Does the Problem Occur?

This problem is usually encountered where *a single standard or generic scale is administered in courses that vary widely in content and instructional methods or formats.* For example, considering the differences in the content, level, format, and size of classes, not all statements may apply to a freshman psychology lecture course of 1,500 students as well as to a doctoral political science seminar with five students. Administering a scale that was designed for an f2f course in an online or blended course can also create a mismatch in coverage and format that can frustrate the students in the online course. Even when one carefully and deliberately generates statements with the intention of creating a "generic" scale, the NA problem may still be unavoidable.

For What Decisions Does the Problem Occur?

Formative decisions.   If the rating scale is being used by professors for formative decisions, and only item-by-item results are presented with the percentage of students picking each anchor, then *the NA option is not a major problem*. Although it is preferable to eliminate the NA option, it is not essential. However, if the ratings will also be employed for summative decisions, the NA problem must be addressed.

Summative decisions.   For summative decisions based on scale or subscale ratings, the NA option's distribution can distort the scale ratings. Every time the option is chosen by any student, his or her scale rating will be different, because one or more items will not be part of the rating. In other words, each rating will be based on different items and cannot be compared or summed with other ratings. This is an analysis nightmare. Freddy Krueger would absolutely love this. *Avoid using the NA option on scales intended for group analysis and summative decisions.* (*NOTE:* This advice would also apply to scale results used for program decisions.)

Observation scales and decisions.   When scales are used for *direct observation of performance and where the ratings to be analyzed involve just a few raters*, such as in peer observation, colleague ratings, administrator ratings, mentor ratings, and self-ratings, it is *permissible to use the NA option*. Such ratings are summarized differently than student ratings are. More judgment may be involved. If a statistical summary is computed, the limitations described previously will still apply.

Two Strategies to Solve the NA Problem

Field-test ID.   One solution rests with attempting to eliminate the source of the problem: evil NA statements. The task is to *identify and then either modify or eliminate the NA statements*. Berk (2006) suggests the following procedure:

1. Field-test the total pool of statements in courses that represent the range of content, structure, level, format, and method characteristics.
2. Include the NA option with the anchor scale.
3. Compute the percentage of students who picked the NA option for every statement.
4. Identify those statements with an NA-response percentage greater than 10%.

5. Assemble a panel of reviewers composed of a sample of the faculty and a few students from the field-tested courses.
6. Ask the panel to explain why the identified statements may be "Not Applicable" to those courses and to suggest how they may be revised to become applicable.
7. Then ask the panel to decide whether to revise or whack the questionable NA statements in order to remove "Not Applicable" as an anchor on the scale.

If the preceding steps were successful in eliminating the NA statements, *there is no need to include the NA option on the final version of the rating scale.* Game, set, match. You win.

Generic scale plus optional subscale.   A second solution to the NA problem is to *develop a "generic" scale applicable to all courses, plus an "optional" subscale* to which each professor can add up to 10 statements related to his or her course only, a common option in commercial scales (see Flashpoints 4 and 10). These course-specific items would allow professors to customize at least a portion of the total scale to the unique characteristics of their courses. The add-on subscale can also provide valuable diagnostic instructional information for professors that would otherwise not be reported on the standard scale.

"Not Observed" (NO) Response

In rating scales based on *direct observation,* "Not Observed" (NO or NOB) indicates *the respondent can't rate the statement because he or she hasn't observed the behavior.* If instead he or she is *not in any position or qualified to answer the statement,* the option may also be expressed as "Unable to Comment" (U/C) or "Unable to Assess" (UA).

This option among the anchors gives respondents an out so they will not feel forced to rate behaviors they have not seen or are not in a position to rate. Picking NO is a good choice. In fact, *raters should be explicitly instructed in the directions for completing the scale to select NO or U/C if appropriate,* so their ratings of the items they do answer are true and honest appraisals of the behaviors they *can* rate. *No score value is assigned to the NO response.* The number of NO responses should be recorded so they can be identified when the scale results are reviewed by the professor for the few peers conducting the observations.

The most common applications of the NO and U/C options are on classroom observation scales. There are frequently items on one observation scale that focus on specific teaching methods and use of technology, and other items that pertain to the professor's content knowledge of the topics being presented. A peer or external reviewer may not have expertise in both teaching methods and the specific teaching content. *Each reviewer should rate only those items for which he or she feels qualified.* The items the reviewer is not qualified to rate should be marked with the NO or U/C anchors. Multiple observers may rate different items on the scale depending on their expertise. *This is the only appropriate strategy to assure reviewers render valid responses by rating only the specific items they are in a position or competent to rate.*

Scoring a Blank (No Response)

What do you do when a student leaves an item blank? "Hmmm, I'm stumped." The blank is different from "Not Applicable" (NA) and "Not Observed" (NO). When students or other raters leave a blankorino, it's not because the statement is NA or NO; it's for some other reason, which I hope I can remember by the time I get to the next paragraph.

What's the Problem?

Item ratings and statistics have to be based on the same sample size (N) for each item in order to compare results from item to item. Otherwise, the mean/median would be calculated on a different number of students for each item, depending on the number of blanks. Usually, there may be only a few blanks on certain items, but *it's best to standardize the N for all analyses.*

When a student skips an item, we don't know why. It could be because

- she wanted to think about the answer a little longer and forgot to go back and answer it,
- he was distracted by the tornado outside and just proceeded to the next item, or
- she experienced an attack of the heebie-jeebies.

Coding a Blank

Imputation rules.   There are numerous "imputation" rules for dealing with missing data on scales. There are at least eight statistical methods described in Allison (2000), Roth (1994), and Rubin (2004), ranging from simple listwise or casewise deletion of students to rather complex techniques I can't even pronounce.

Because maximizing the student response rate for every course, especially those with small Ns, is super important, according to Flashpoint 6, a rule has to be chosen. Deletion of missing responses by choosing either *listwise or casewise deletion* will reduce the response rate. Bad decision! Bad, bad decision! Try again. *Mean substitution* for each blank also is inappropriate because of the probable bias from the skewed distributions (see Flashpoint 9).

Missing indicator method. The simplest strategy that will not alter the response rate is to *assign the midpoint quantitative value to the missing response.* Yup, that's what I said. This is known as the *missing indicator* method (Guan & Yusoff, 2011). "How do you do that?" Before any analysis is conducted or ratings computed, make the following adjustments based on the number of options on the scale:

- *Odd-numbered scale* (containing a midpoint anchor): A blank is assigned a 2 on a five-point scale (0–4) or 3 on a seven-point scale (0–6).
- *Even-numbered scale* (without a midpoint anchor): A blank is assigned a 1.5 on a four-point scale (0–3) or 2.5 on a 6-point scale (0–5).

Once you have converted the blanks on the scale to the appropriate midpoint values, you can calculate the item ratings.

This strategy *assumes the respondent had no opinion on the behavior being rated or couldn't make a choice* on the item and, therefore, left it blank. The blank is considered to be equivalent to a neutral response. This is a reasonable assumption for the few cases that may occur. If blanks appear with regularity on specific items, it's possible those items may be NA or NO. Those items should be examined carefully to assure that all respondents can answer them. If not, then they may need to be revised (the items, not the respondents).

Recommendations

The four escape responses to rating scale items must be addressed to accurately compute any of the ratings and report the results (Berk, 2006). Carefully review your scoring process to make sure these responses are considered when the analyses are performed. Here is a recap:

1. *Eliminate the "Neutral" anchor* from all rating scales measuring teaching effectiveness.

2. *Use the "Not Applicable" anchor during the field test* to identify, and then revise or discard, NA items on the student rating scale. The NA option should not appear on the final version. The NA option is permissible on scales used by professors for formative decisions and on peer observation and other scales rated by a few individuals, but not by groups.

3. *Include the "Not Observed" anchor in observation scales* to pinpoint those items the rater could not observe or the *"Unable to Comment" anchor* for items the rater would not be qualified to rate. The NO or U/C option does not receive a rating value in scoring.

4. A *blank,* or nonresponse to an item, on student rating scales can wreak havoc with the scoring process unless the "blank" is assigned a numerical value. It *can be treated as a neutral response and, therefore, assigned a midpoint value* on the scale being used, either even or odd numbers. This adjustment will automatically set the number of items used in the scoring to the same total for all students to maximize response rate.

11

FLASHPOINT 9

Criterion-Referenced vs. Norm-Referenced
Rating Interpretations

When you compute the score on any rating scale, how do you interpret it? This is one of the most confusing issues. The rating means nothing by itself. For student rating scales, one of the selling points of the commercial scale and scoring packages is the national norms the vendors provide for comparing an institution's ratings to the ratings of professors who teach similar courses at loads of other colleges. That tells individual professors and administrators how they stack up against others. That's interesting, but what do you do with that information? This section will attempt to clarify the various options for interpreting ratings on scales used to measure teaching effectiveness. Because these ratings are used for summative (employment) decisions, steps to avoid costly litigation involving U.S. EEOC Guidelines *for "adverse impact" will also be suggested.*

Rating Referencing

Asingle rating from any scale at any level has no intrinsic meaning by itself; it's just a number. *A rating of 2 or 15 or 90 has to be referenced to something to have meaning.* It can be referenced to the job content domain defining effective teaching; the possible score range for the item, subscale, or scale; a standard (cutoff score) of performance; and/or norm group performance (Berk, 1984). The issue of what this reference point should be to evaluate teaching effectiveness has been debated in the literature for more than 20 years (Abrami, 2001; Aleamoni, 1996; Cashin, 1992, 1994, 1996; Hativa, 1993; McKeachie, 1996; Theall, 1996). Let's examine each of these reference points.

Mean Rating Bias in Skewed Distributions

The simple choice between using the mean or the median (i.e., midpoint) for the item, subscale, and total scale rating statistics is very important. This is because *the MEAN misrepresents the actual ratings in a negatively skewed distribution* by being oversensitive to the few extremely low ratings. That hypersensitivity gets the mean into trouble. Those ratings lower the mean, thereby distorting a professor's class rating when most students may have rated him or her very highly. *This bias makes a professor appear worse* than the ratings actually indicate. *Allowing a professor to be portrayed as a less effective teacher with lower ratings due to statistical bias is indefensible.*

Mean vs. Median Ratings in Score Reports

Although the median is less discriminating as an index, it is more accurate, more representative, and less biased than the mean under this distribution condition. Based on the skewness of the distribution and the ordinality of the Likert-type rating scale, *the MEDIAN is the most appropriate measure of central tendency* (Berk, 2006). The lower the degree of skew, the more similar both measures will be. In a perfectly normal distribution, the mean and median are identical. However, because ratings of faculty, administrators, courses, programs, ice cream, movie stars, political candidates, and everything else are typically skewed, *it is highly recommended that BOTH measures of central tendency be reported.* If you're using vendor-generated online reports, check on the options available.

Criterion-Referenced Interpretations

Although the Likert-type graphic rating scale was designed to produce a total rating across all items, there are several levels of rating other than the total scale that can provide useful information. In fact, there are at least *four possible levels of rating interpretation* that have built-in standards or benchmarks for performance:

1. Item anchor
2. Item

3. Subscale
4. Total scale

These are generic levels applicable to most of the rating scales used to measure teaching effectiveness. These levels furnish the summary information bites (*NOTE TO EDITOR:* Or is it "bytes"?) for the decisions that follow. (*NOTE TO AUTHOR:* "You're driving me crazy! I don't care. Nobody will read this far into the book, anyway.")

Formative Decisions

For faculty who need data to improve their teaching, the most appropriate diagnostic information provided by rating scales is at the *anchor and item levels* on the structured part of the scale and the compiled students' comments or answers on the unstructured part. Here is a simple presentation of anchor and item results for three statements on a rating scale:

	SD	D	A	SA	*N*	Mean	Median
Statement 1	1.0%	3.1%	37.5%	58.6%	96	2.52	3.00
Statement 2	1.0	3.1	24.0	71.9	96	2.65	3.00
Statement 3	1.1	1.1	28.9	68.9	90	2.57	3.00

Anchor level percentages.   This mini-report displays an *anchor distribution* of the percentage of students picking each anchor, item by item. The anchor abbreviations for "Strongly Disagree" (SD), "Disagree" (D), "Agree" (A), and "Strongly Agree" (SA) are listed horizontally, left to right, *from unfavorable to favorable* ratings. *N* is the number of students that responded to the statement, which was the same for the first two items but lower for the third.

The percentages for the four anchors indicate the percentage distribution based on the actual number of responders. *A professor can obtain a criterion-referenced interpretation of these percentages by simply referencing them to the anchors.* For example, a professor would expect low percentages for the first two "Disagree" anchors and high percentages for the second two "Agree" anchors, with the highest for SA. The percentages taper off drastically from right to left, with tiny percentages for D and SD for all three items. Those low percentages create the skewness in the distributions and lower the mean ratings to the right. (*NOTE:* The percentages are slightly different for statement 3 compared to statements 1 and 2, particularly the 1.1 percent who chose D. This was due, in part, to the six fewer students who responded to that item [*N* = 90].)

This overall response pattern is an example of the *negatively skewed distribution* of responses mentioned previously, which is the most common outcome. *It occurs when the majority of the responses are A and SA, but there is also a sprinkling of a few Ds and SDs.* The extreme SD responses, or "outliers," create the skew. Realistically, a few students might mark "SD" for every statement to express their desire to see the professor smacked, hacked, or whacked; however, the majority of satisfied customers will choose the two higher, more positive "Agree" anchors.

This basic information provides the professor with *the most detailed profile of responses to a single item.* The percentages reveal the degree of agreement and disagreement with each statement. It is diagnostic of how the class felt about each behavior or characteristic. The professor can then *consider specific changes in teaching, evaluation, or course behaviors* to shift the distribution farther to the right, into the A–SA zone, the next time the class is taught. The rating percentages gain meaning just by referencing them to the anchors.

Item-level means/medians. The *item means* and *medians* to the right of the anchor distribution summarize the responses to each item with a single number based on a four-point scale with the anchors coded from 0 through 3. For simplicity and interpretability, *a zero-based scale is recommended,* in which the most negative anchor (e.g., SD) is coded as "0," and the other anchors are coded in one-point increments above 0. This coding was originally recommended by Likert (1932).

This zero-base coding should be applied to the subscales and total scale as well for consistency. The zero base for all score interpretations is easy to remember: *the worst, most unfavorable rating on any item, subscale, or total scale is "0."* What changes in each subscale is the upper rating limit for the most favorable rating because the number of items is different.

Because the item means/medians in the previous example are based on the total N for the class, they can be referenced to benchmarks on the quantitative scale. For example, at minimum, on a scale of 0 to 3, *means at and above 1.5 and medians at and above 2 indicate strengths; those below the midpoint (1.5) denote weaknesses.* Notice that *all means are lower than the respective medians due to the skewness.* That is fairly common for most results. The means/medians in conjunction with the anchor percentages provide meaningful diagnostic information to red flag—or orange cone—areas that might need attention. Again, this report is intended for the professor's use primarily, but the results on course characteristics may have curricular implications.

Once the anchor and item results have been analyzed, *the list of students' comments should be reviewed.* For paper-based administrations, this list may be relatively short; for online, it may take up several pages per question depending on the size of the class. The comments should be related to the ratings. Often, the comments explain the high or low ratings on specific items, which can be helpful in suggesting what types of changes might be considered.

Summative Decisions

For decisions made by an administrator or promotion-and-tenure committee, *summary ratings are needed across several courses for a year (for an annual review) or three or more years (for a promotion review).* If the items on the total scale are grouped into clusters related to topics such as instructional methods, evaluation methods, and course content, the item ratings can be summed to produce subscale scores. Items can also be grouped into "Course" and "Instructor" composite subscales. The *Standards* (AERA, APA, & NCME Joint Committee on Standards, 1999) require that *these ratings only be used for decision making if adequate reliability and validity evidence, such as reliability coefficients and factor analysis results, support that internal scale structure* (Standards 1.12 and 2.7). Because each subscale contains a different number of items, the rating range will also be different. This range must be reported to interpret the results.

Subscale and scale-level ratings.   Total scale, course-and-instructor-composites, and subscale ratings are the most appropriate levels of reporting for summative decisions. Each midpoint and highest rating is computed by multiplying the point value of an item (1.5 for midpoint and 3 for highest rating) by the number of items. Notice the zero-base "Extremely Unfavorable" rating for all subscales and the total.

As shown in the following subscales (see p. 78), the criterion-referenced interpretation of the results is analogous to the item results, only the numbers are bigger. For example, instead of a range of 0 to 3 and a midpoint of 1.5 for an item, each subscale has a range and midpoint based on its respective number of items.

*Midpoint and upper-limit standards.   *Once the means/medians are computed for all the subscales and total scale, *they can be referenced initially to the midpoint ratings and the upper-limit or maximum rating to identify strong and weak areas.* So, for Subscale 4 with 13 items, the mean and median can

	Extremely Unfavorable	Midpoint	Extremely Favorable
Subscale 1 (8 items)	0 ————————	12 ————————	24
Subscale 2 (5 items)	0 ————————	7.5 ————————	15
Subscale 3 (4 items)	0 ————————	6 ————————	12
Subscale 4 (13 items)	0 ————————	19.5 ————————	39
Subscale 5 (6 items)	0 ————————	9 ————————	18
Course (16 items)	0 ————————	24 ————————	48
Instructor (20 items)	0 ————————	30 ————————	60
Total Scale (36 items)	0 ————————	54 ————————	108

be referenced to the midpoint of 19.5 and upper limit of 39 to locate their positions on the following continuum:

Continuum for Subscale 4

Extremely Unfavorable	Midpoint	Mean 34.79	Extremely Favorable
0—————————————	—19.5———————	——————⌐	—39
		Median 37	

The mean/median ratings on Subscale 4 rock (aka "Very Favorable"). The skewed distribution accounts for the lower mean compared to median.

Third-quarter standard.   It is also possible to layer another criterion-referenced benchmark on this continuum that is more stringent than just a comparison to the midpoint and maximum "Extremely Favorable" rating. The scale continuum has built-in benchmarks based on the four anchors. For example, one can easily *partition any rating scale into quarters* and choose 75% as the cutoff rating. That would mean that all faculty members should attain a 75% "Favorable" (F) rating or above (in our example, 81 out of 108 points, or 36 items × 0–3 point scale), as opposed to 25% "Unfavorable" (U), on the total scale and on all subscales in their courses. The range on the total scale is from 0 (36 × 0) to 108 (36 × 3).

How do those benchmarks translate into each subscale continuum? The following five subscales are chopped into quarters:

Subscale	EU	U	Mdpt.	F	EF
Subscale 1	0.00	6.00	12.00	18.00	24.00
Subscale 2	0.00	3.75	7.50	11.25	15.00
Subscale 3	0.00	3.00	6.00	9.00	12.00
Subscale 4	0.00	9.75	19.50	29.25	39.00
Subscale 5	0.00	4.50	9.00	13.50	18.00
Total	0.00	27.00	54.00	81.00	108.00
Grade	F	D	C	B	A

The ratings at each quarter position on the scale provide additional reference points for interpretation of performance. You can even assign *criterion-referenced letter grades* to that performance. The specification of any criteria for performance must be agreed on by the faculty.

Standard setting. It is in the process of picking criteria where faculty and administrators need to be careful. Despite its intuitive appeal, standard setting in this rating scale application can be arbitrary. How do you choose the standard? It seems simple enough. Just look at the score range and select a point. However, this *cardiac approach* to standard setting ("I know in my heart that a total scale rating of 81/108, or 75%, indicates effective teaching") is not acceptable, nor is it defensible according to the *Standards* (AERA, APA, & NCME Joint Committee on Standards, 1999). For faculty or an administrator to set a standard this way is arbitrary and capricious.

What is a reasonable approach? Assemble a *faculty committee* to systematically consider cutoff ratings on the total scale and various subscales. There are more than 50 systematic judgmental procedures this committee could follow to arrive at *realistic, defensible standards for teaching performance* (see Berk, 1986, 1996; Cizek, 2001). According to Standards 4.20 and 4.21, such methods are essential if high-stakes summative decisions by administrators will be made about faculty based on those standards. However, student ratings alone should not be used for merit pay and promotion decisions. Other indicators of performance from multiple sources of evidence should be taken into account (Standard 14.13).

Legal warning for administrators. In Flashpoint 7 on global ratings, the importance of the cutoff rating for summative decisions and the resulting "impact" on minority and protected groups were described. They bear mentioning again in this context. There are federal laws that protect employees in higher education from various forms of discrimination. Those laws include Title VII of the Civil Rights Act of 1964, Title IX of the Education Amendments of 1972, and the Equal Pay Act of 1963, plus the U.S. Equal Employment Opportunity Commission's *Uniform Guidelines on Employee Selection Procedures* (U.S. Code of Federal Regulations, 1978).

- *Title VII:* Prohibits public and private employers from discriminating based on race, color, religion, sex, or national origin. U.S.C. § 2000e-2(a)(1) (2000).
- *Title IX:* Prohibits gender discrimination in educational programs and in activities receiving federal funds. U.S.C. §§ 1681–1688 (2000).
- *Equal Pay Act:* Prohibits employers from paying lower wages to one gender for "equal work on jobs the performance of which require equal skill, effort, and responsibility, and which are performed under similar working conditions," with exceptions for wage differentials based on factors other than sex. U.S.C. § 206(d)(1) (2000).

For administrators and faculty serving on promotion and tenure committees, here are three major considerations to avoid costly litigation (Is there any other kind?) on decisions made using the student rating scale and other measures:

1. *Cutoff ratings:* Administrators are not permitted to (a) adjust the ratings of any professor; (b) use different cutoff ratings for different faculty based on age, gender, race, ethnicity, or any other protected class; or (c) alter the results to discriminate against a particular group (U.S. EEOC, 2010).
2. *Adverse impact and the "80/20 rule":* Because student ratings, along with other measures of teaching performance, can be used to hire, promote, demote, or fire a part-time or full-time faculty member (Wines & Lau, 2006), *administrators should record data on their faculty by EEOC-protected category in order to demonstrate that the rating scales do not have "adverse impact."*

   They should *apply the 80/20 rule to ensure the scale is not discriminatory.* Accumulating decisions on faculty over a year or more, a department chair should find that minority faculty meet or exceed the rating cutoff at least 80% as often as majority faculty. For example, if the student rating scale were administered to all medical faculty, and say, 60% of White male faculty met the 75% total rating cutoff, at least 48% (.80 × 60%) of minority women faculty must also have met the cutoff for the scale to be considered non-discriminatory.

This rule was illustrated in the gender discrimination case of *Farrell v. Butler University* (Chase, 2007) involving denial of an academic award and unequal pay. Five years of student ratings along with loads of other evidence were presented on behalf of the plaintiff.

3. *Psychometric studies:* More than 80 appeals and district court cases on employment testing (Ashe & U.S. EEOC, 2007) indicate that any instrument used for personnel decisions under the U.S. EEOC *Guidelines* must have adequate technical evidence of reliability and validity, including a comprehensive job analysis of the job's tasks related to a person's knowledge, skills, and abilities (KSAs). This *emphasizes the importance of documented psychometric studies of student rating scales and all other measures of teaching effectiveness* to support their use for summative decisions (Wines & Lau, 2006).

Criterion-referenced interpretation of rating scale scores can be meaningful for administrative decisions about teaching performance and curriculum committee decisions of course effectiveness. However, the validity and fairness of those decisions hinge on the method used to select the criteria and the supplemental evidence beyond those scores that is considered to make the individual or course decisions. Caution should be observed in the process of arriving at criterion-referenced interpretations to assure they are fair and equitable in the context to which they are applied.

Norm-Referenced Interpretations

Beyond all the information and criterion-referenced interpretations possible for making formative and summative decisions described in the preceding section, you can add more ratings, from specific groups of courses and faculty, for norm-referenced interpretations. All *criterion-referenced ratings are collected and compared WITHIN each course*, but all *norm groups and comparisons are OUTSIDE of the course*, thereby furnishing a different frame of reference and new information. Normative comparisons may be of interest to individual faculty, administrators at different levels, and curriculum committees. However, *under no conditions should faculty be ranked by their course ratings to hundredths of a decimal point according to any norms* (Wines & Lau, 2006).

Norm Group Composition and Selection

Academic norms.   Any group can serve as a norm group or sample to which ratings are referenced. It is critical that the choice of the norm be a *fair and equitable comparison group*. Although the most legitimate direct norm might be similar courses or disciplines at the same program level, department and school composites also tend to be common norms. The most meaningful norms are department, program (baccalaureate, master's, or doctoral level), school, college, university, region (e.g., consortium of colleges), and nation, as well as conglomerate, cartel, continent, hemisphere, planet, and constellation. Who wouldn't want to know how his or her statistics course stacks up against an alien stats course on Mars?

Demographic norms.   Ratings can be aggregated at those different levels and also subgrouped into certain demographic categories by professor characteristics, such as rank, gender, ethnicity, age, height, BMI, hair color, and girth, and by course characteristics, such as title or subject matter, level (baccalaureate, master's, or doctoral level), format (f2f, blended/hybrid, or online), scheduling (day, evening, or weekend), class size, and so on. Virtually any combination of courses can serve as a norm. Given the validity studies on many of these characteristics (see reviews by Benton & Cashin, 2012; Nilson, 2012), a professor's performance as compared to these norm groups may be very informative.

Commercial scale norms.   Commercial online administration and student-rating-scale packages (see Flashpoint 4) provide several norm options, including national, usually in the form of means and standard deviations. A few vendors report graphic formats of percentile ranks. The various norms those vendors offer can provide a perspective and directions for identifying strengths and weaknesses in teaching and course structure, particularly at the item and subscale levels.

"Home-grown" scale norms.   Back in Neverland, even though "home-grown" scale ratings cannot be referenced to national norms, regional norms may be possible. If the same rating scale is used at several state-sponsored colleges or universities, for example, statewide norms can be generated by subject and program level. Alternatively, private institutions that are members of a consortium of schools in the same region may agree on a common scale that can be administered to compute regional norms.

Longitudinal norms. Norm-group ratings can also be used to set a baseline teaching performance against which future ratings can be compared longitudinally for semester, annual, and multiyear evaluations. A trend analysis can provide evidence of teaching and course improvements or decrements over time. This evidence would be appropriate for summative individual decisions annually and for promotion and tenure review. Program-level scores with norms can be reported in accreditation documents.

Interpretation of Norms

Any norm of your choice provides *the relative position of any professor, course, or other aggregate ratings in relation to a relevant group.* In addition to the means/medians for all the items, subscales, and total scale displayed for criterion-referenced interpretations, *means/medians* and, sometimes, *percentile ranks* would also be reported for each norm group chosen. Those statistics *permit observations of above or below norms, degree of differences, and rank.* That provides jugs of information to interpret. Be extremely careful with ranks.

Formative decisions. How much data does a professor need for formative decisions? Anchor percentages and item means/medians supply extremely detailed statistics for a professor to pinpoint specific areas that should be given attention. For teaching and course improvement, *within-course diagnostic information* is the most valuable. Criterion-referenced interpretations of structured items and qualitative analysis of the unstructured comments furnish the appropriate guide to specific improvements.

So how can norms help detect problems in a course? *Outside-course item-by-item means/medians from norms on similar courses* can provide comparisons to corroborate areas of strength, identify similar areas of weakness or difficulty, and isolate areas of discrepancy that should be reviewed further. The norms give an external perspective that would not be available otherwise.

Summative decisions. How much data does a department chair need for summative decisions? For example, a graphic display or format of your choosing of rating results for contract renewal would require subscale and total scale means/medians for all the professor's courses for the past year plus those for the department, college, and any other norm group. It's important that course subject matter and program level be matched with the norm characteristics as closely as possible.

What do these norm comparisons add beyond the criterion-referenced comparisons? They indicate whether the professor's ratings are above or below the norms and to what degree. His or her *relative positions across courses may be reviewed for consistency or inconsistency in performance along with the criterion-referenced interpretations and evidence from self, peer, and other sources* to reach a decision. Although the decision may be made without normative comparisons, the norms provide the different dimension and outside-course perspective that are meaningful in interpreting the ratings. These are comparisons for an individual professor across courses and over time, not across professors.

Another legal warning for administrators.   As noted at the beginning of this section, *administrators should NOT rank faculty based on any set of norms for pay, retention, or promotion decisions.* Ranks using course ratings to hundredths of a decimal point from student rating scales are unfair, biased, and indefensible. According to Wines and Lau (2006), those ranks could produce evidence of "disparate impact" against one or more protected groups, which means *the scale might discriminate particularly against women, Asians, and older faculty.* For example, "normed ratings" expressed as ranks would violate the Equal Pay Act of 1963, described previously, if they are used as the single data source to distribute either merit or discretionary pay. Those ratings can discriminate based on gender, race, or ethnicity.

Recommendations

Interpretation of ratings from student rating scales as well as other measures is essential for decision making. So what are your options? Always start with the decisions.

Formative Decisions

The most appropriate ratings for pinpointing areas that need improvement are the percentage distribution across the anchors and the item means/medians. The *anchor and item levels provide the most specific, detailed information* to determine what aspects of the course or teaching methods need attention. The *subscale means/medians can also provide a diagnostic profile of strengths and weaknesses.*

An individual professor's rating of below the criterion of, for example, 75% may identify a red-flag area. Certainly anything below 50% would be cause for concern. Ratings below department or similar course norms would also be red flags. *Student comments should also be analyzed in conjunction with the red-flag items to explain those poor responses.* The comments can be extremely illuminating and guide specific teaching and course changes.

Summative Decisions

Annual and promotion-and-tenure-committee reviews require the *display of total ratings of courses over a year or several years,* such as time in rank. That rating profile may be referenced to the department criterion and norms at the departmental, regional, and national levels, where available. Course ratings that consistently exceed departmental and regional or national norms for similar courses may be very helpful in assessing teaching effectiveness for summative decisions. Another normative comparison is growth in ratings over time. The trends across multiple years should be indicative of improvement or a marked decline in teaching quality. *Administrators should document all decisions to assure the 80/20 rule for adverse impact is met. Decisions about faculty should NOT be based on any ranks or normed ratings.*

Program Decisions

The overall effectiveness and improvement in teaching by program level, department, or discipline year after year can be measured by student ratings at the subscale and total scale levels. *Annual mean/median norms by semester* can furnish the results. This may reveal trends in teaching effectiveness over a five-year period, for example, that may be attributable to particular faculty development and innovative teaching programs. *Course composite ratings and subscales dealing with course characteristics may be analyzed by curriculum committees* to suggest possible content or organizational revisions. Item and subscale means/medians can guide such reviews.

For further information on rating interpretation, including several examples, please see Berk (2006, chapter 9).

12

FLASHPOINT 10

Face-to-Face vs. Online Course Rating Scales

All the preceding flashpoints and recommendations focused on student rating scales and other sources of evidence designed expressly for f2f courses. Can they be used with online courses? Aren't those courses structured and delivered differently than f2f courses? Isn't the use of technology a big factor that should be measured? Do you now need to develop all new measures for the online courses? Ruminate over that. In fact, try breathing into a paper bag. Are you getting chest pain? You'll be okay. Oh, and one more thought: What about blended/hybrid courses? This is the monkey-wrench flashpoint.

Status of Online Courses

The Pew Research Center's survey of U.S. colleges and universities found that more than 75% offer online courses (Parker, Lenhart, & Moore, 2011). More than 30% of all college enrollments in fall 2010 were in online courses (Allen & Seaman, 2011) and nearly 9% of all graduate degrees in 2008 were earned online (Wei et al., 2009).

The conversion of traditional f2f courses into either blended/hybrid combinations of f2f and online or into fully online courses is increasing at a NASCAR pace, along with enrollments in those courses. Further, there is no sign of these trends abating nationally (APLU/Sloan National Commission on Online Learning, 2009), internationally (Strategy Group, 2011), or galactically (Still Looking for Reference, in press). Distance education in all of its forms is the "course tsunami" of the future. Watch out! Everyone needs to be prepared.

Unfortunately, *the evaluation of these courses lags far behind their development in terms of available measures, quality of measures, and delivery systems* (Hathorn & Hathorn, 2010; Rothman, Romeo, Brennan, & Mitchell, 2011). The recent *Survey of Distance Learning Programs in Higher Education* (Primary Research Group, 2012), which looked at colleges in the United States, Canada, and the United Kingdom, found that fewer than 20% of the colleges (15% U.S. and 37.5% CA and UK) have at least one full-time staff person devoted to evaluating the online distance learning program.

What's the Problem?

Comparisons of f2f and online courses yield mixed results. There are certain common characteristics but also unique elements in each type of course. How are you supposed to evaluate these "different" types of courses?

Common Characteristics

A brief review of the research by Benton and Cashin (2012) and a more extensive review by Drouin (2012) both came to the same conclusion: *F2f and online courses are more similar than they are different.* They share several key "teaching factors" in common, such as course organization, communication of information, facilitating learning, and student assessment (Wang, Dziuban, Cook, & Moskal, 2009).

Drouin (2012) identified five criteria of *"best practices" in online courses* that she says could serve as best practices in f2f as well. The categories of those criteria are (1) student–student and student–instructor interactions, (2) instructor support and mentoring, (3) lecture/content-delivery quality, (4) course content, and (5) course structure (p. 69). The differences lie in the use of technology related to the delivery of content and social networking tools.

Unique Characteristics of Online Courses

In contrast to Drouin's criteria, Creasman (2012) extracted *seven key differences in online courses*:

1. Asynchronous activity, where students can interact with each other and course materials anytime, 24/7
2. Non-linear discussions on message boards and forums, where students can participate in multiple conversations simultaneously

3. Communication primarily via written text
4. Slower communication between instructor and students, primarily via e-mail
5. Greater social contact and time spent by instructor with students on website
6. Greater volume of information and resources available
7. Instructor's roles as a facilitator, "guide on the side," and also co-learner (p. 2)

So what do these differences mean in terms of the scales you use to measure teaching in the online courses? Can these differences be covered on new scales, or should current f2f scales be administered in online courses? That's the problem tackled in the next section.

Seven Strategies to Evaluate Teaching Effectiveness in Online Courses

As online courses have been developed following different models of teaching (Anderson & Dron, 2011; Creasman, 2012; Peltier, Schibrowsky, & Drago, 2007), existing traditional f2f rating scales have been challenged in regard to their application to these courses (Harrington & Reasons, 2005; Loveland, 2007). The f2f approach to scales has often seemed efficient because many of those student rating scales were already being administered online at hundreds of institutions. This administration was being executed either by an in-house IT system or by an out-house vendor specializing in online administration, analysis, and score reporting, such as CollegeNET, ConnectEDU, EvaluationKIT, or IOTA Solutions (see Flashpoint 4 for details).

Despite these online capabilities in place at many colleges and universities, it has become apparent that *f2f measures might NOT address all of the essential components of online teaching* (Loveland, 2007). This validity issue seriously questions the actual coverage of instructor behaviors and course characteristics. Perhaps new measures are needed that are tailored to the specific features of those courses.

A review of the research and current practices in evaluating f2f and online courses suggest there are at least seven options for measuring teaching effectiveness in online and blended courses (Berk, 2013a):

1. Instructor-Developed Scales

"Encourage instructor-developed scales to evaluate online teaching and courses." Are you kidding me? Some institutions have placed the responsibility for evaluating the online course on the individual instructor or simply neglect the evaluation (Compora, 2003). Unless instructors are trained in the process of scale construction and score analysis and interpretation for formative or summative decisions, this should not even be considered as an option. Further, with increased faculty teaching loads and other tasks tacked on to instructors' job descriptions because of budget cuts or other reasons, it doesn't seem fair to add another task, one for which they are probably not qualified.

Although with free online survey providers, such as *Zoomerang* (Market-Tools, 2006), and several others (Wright, 2005), the technology exists to easily administer online course scales of up to 30 items per scale via e-mail (Hong, 2008), it is not recommended. Further, after all that has been learned in the evaluation of f2f courses, the complexity of multiple measures, such as student, self, peer, administrator, and mentor rating scales, cannot be handled by every instructor. *Online course evaluation should not be the job of the instructor.* There are much better ways to do it.

2. Traditional Face-to-Face Student Rating Scale

"Use the traditional student rating scale and other measures that are currently in operation for the f2f courses." This is not an uncommon practice for student scales (Beattie, Spooner, Jordan, Algozzine, & Spooner, 2002; Compora, 2003)—particularly when you use a double negative in a sentence—but may not be generalizable to self, peer, and other measures.

Studies using the *IDEA Student Ratings of Instruction* form *in both types of courses yield comparable ratings* on several items, including course and instructor global items (Benton et al., 2010a). Also, there were similar item means, internal consistency reliabilities, and factor structures (McGee & Lowell, 2003), and nearly identical overall ratings of the instructor (Wang & Newlin, 2000).

This continuation of the *f2f scale administration to all courses will not capture elements that are unique to each type of course* as well as the specific emphases and concentration in delivery methods and technology that may be especially useful for course design and improvement. Student feedback on the total package, not part of it, would be preferable. The remaining options make that possible.

3. Optional Items Added to Face-to-Face Scale

"Use 10 optional items on the f2f traditional scale to measure the online characteristics." This may be the *most efficient and cost-effective approach* to retain those items in common to both f2f and online courses, but also add items to measure the uses of technology and other aspects of teaching that are different for online courses.

Consider a *10-item optional subscale tacked onto the "generic" f2f scale.* This subscale is usually built into many "home-grown" scales constructed by faculty committees in-house as well as most of the commercially developed scale packages (see Flashpoint 4). In f2f courses, these 10 course-specific items would permit instructors to customize at least a portion of the total scale to the unique characteristics of their respective courses. However, in online and blended/hybrid courses, *the 10 items would be a specifically designed standard set of online items measuring technology and other topics,* which would be the same for all online courses. Psychometric analysis would have to be conducted on this subscale to establish reliability and validity.

A major advantage of this option is the norms available for various score comparisons. Depending on the system design, there may be local, regional, and national norms. This scale configuration would *allow comparisons between f2f and online courses on the same "generic" scale and also between online and blended courses on the 10-item "online" subscale.* That feedback would provide valuable information for formative, summative, and program decisions.

4. Revision of Face-to-Face Scale

"Adapt or revise the current scales to fit the online courses." This is an extension of the preceding strategy to be employed when the 10-item add-on subscale is not adequate. If more items are required to cover online teaching, then this option suggested by Tallent-Runnels and colleagues (Tallent-Runnels et al., 2006) may be your option. They attached a "technology evaluation" to an existing scale.

The add-on subscales measuring characteristics and teaching behaviors in an online environment may also be used in blended/hybrid courses. As with the preceding option, the new items and subscales would require item analysis, reliability, and validity studies to compare their psychometric quality with the rest of the scale.

5. New Rating Scales

"Develop new rating scales for online courses." This "throw-the-baby-out . . ." approach may be the *most time-consuming and costly option,* plus it may not

be necessary for student rating scales. Building new measures from scratch intended solely for online courses is not without precedent. Several examples for constructing self and peer rating scales to fit three models of online teaching (i.e., cognitive behavioral, social-constructivism, and connectivism) at half a dozen institutions are described by Drouin (2012).

6. Commercially Developed Student Rating Scale

"Use one of the commercially developed online scales already available." Among the seven commercial packages described in Flashpoint 4, *only two out-house vendors market scales that are designed expressly for online courses*: (1) *e-SIR*, which is a 41-item scale with half of the items from the *Student Instructional Report II* (*SIR II*) by Educational Testing Service, and (2) a 31-item distance learning form from the *Instructional Assessment System* (*IAS Online*) at the Office of Educational Assessment, University of Washington. Neither vendor reports any reliability coefficients or validity evidence on its website. These scales should be examined carefully by directors of distance education programs for their content coverage compared to that of the published scales described next. There are major differences to consider.

7. Published Student Rating Scale

(*EDITOR:* Please insert drumroll.) This is the final option: *"Use available published scales constructed expressly for online courses."* There are also resources available at other institutions that can assist in adopting, adapting, or developing online scales (Hathorn & Hathorn, 2010; Hosie, Schibeci, & Backhaus, 2005; Quality Matters, 2007).

There are three published student rating scales identified by Drouin (2012) that are worthy of review. Perhaps these scales will inspire the additions indicated in the preceding options.

1. *Student Evaluation of Online Teaching Effectiveness* (*SEOTE*) (Bangert, 2006, 2008): A 26-item, Likert-type "Agree–Disagree" six-point scale specifically aligned with Chickering and Gamson's (1987) seven principles of effective teaching; a large portion of the items can be used in f2f courses as well; has high reliability with four interpretable factors (i.e., student–faculty interaction, active learning, time on task, and cooperation among students)

2. *Student Evaluation of Web-Based Instruction* (*SEWBI*) (Stewart, Hong, & Strudler, 2004): A lengthy, very comprehensive 59-item Likert-type "Agree–Disagree" five-point scale with a very heavy

emphasis on the technological aspects of the course and use of multi-media; moderate to high reliability (.75–.85 for all subscales except technical issues, which is .92); factor analysis and results reported in seven dimensions (i.e., appearance of websites, hyperlinks and navigation, technical issues, online applications, class procedures and expectations, content delivery, and instructor and peer interaction)

3. *Students' Perceptions of Online Courses* (*SPOC*) (Rothman et al., 2011): A 25-item, Likert-type "Agree–Disagree" five-point scale that covers both general and specific behaviors mostly appropriate for online courses; high reliability, with items distributed across six factors (i.e., appropriateness of readings/assignments, technological tools, instructor feedback and communication, course organization, clarity of outcomes and requirements, and content format); supplements the *SIR II* scale administered to f2f courses

Recommendations

Online courses are sprouting up on campuses worldwide. Unfortunately, at some institutions evaluations of those courses haven't even been planted yet. After they are planted, directors of distance education probably will not be sure exactly what they should look like. The preceding review suggests a state-of-the-art "consumer's guide" to the evaluation of online and blended courses. Let the "evaluation sprouting" begin!

Should Uniqueness of Online Courses Be Measured?

Despite the similarity of ratings in f2f and online courses with traditional f2f scales, the *unique characteristics of online courses should be measured to furnish a more complete, as opposed to a biased, evaluation of those courses.* The issue is how to do that efficiently and cost-effectively to produce psychometrically defensible scales.

Conclusion

The seven options presented in this chapter are worthy of consideration. Options 3, 4, 6, and 7 seem to have the greatest potential for student rating scales. Option 5 will probably be necessary in order for self, peer, and other rating scales to provide a comprehensive assessment of online teaching effectiveness. Those multiple measures are essential in order to furnish the evidence needed (a) by faculty for formative decisions to improve their teaching; (b) by administrators for summative decisions on contract renewal, merit pay, promotion and tenure, and teaching awards; and (c) by directors of distance education for program decisions.

Further research is required to empirically evaluate the efficacy, efficiency, cost-effectiveness, and psychometric soundness of the preceding options as they are implemented. There is no simple solution or generic model that will fit every institution's online-course evaluation needs. As with f2f applications, appropriate rating scales and other measures of teaching effectiveness must be tailored to the specific courses (online or blended), faculty, students, culture, and resources at each institution. The seven options suggested in this chapter provide tentative strategies to consider.

TOP 10 RECOMMENDATIONS

S o, what are the takeaways? There are no goody bags. This isn't a party. However, we have progressed—from "Fractured Fairy Tales" in the kickoff chapter to looping response rates in Flashpoint 6 to online course sprouting in Flashpoint 10. This has certainly been an exciting, occasionally informative, and moderately amusing journey.

After reading one or more flashpoints, . . . Wait! I bet some of you didn't read any and just skipped to the end, thinking this was an Agatha Christie–type mystery. Well, did you solve the mystery or identify the grammatical structure of the previous sentence, with its dangling flashpoints? (*ANSWER:* This is a rarely used structure, known only to a few English scholars, called an "invective marsupial.") We now move on to the next paragraph, because this one is battered beyond recognition. Sorry for any inconvenience.

What Are the Takeaways?

We Have Issues!

After scratching your head over the preceding paragraph and the flashpoints you've processed, it's reasonable to conclude, "We have issues!" The 10 flashpoints covered are just a starting point. You have probably thought of many more that need attention. Remember what Leonardo DiCaprio said to Kate Winslet in *Titanic*? "Rose, why do I have to get wet and freeze like a Popsicle?" (*READER QUERY:* "What does that quote have to do with the topic of this paragraph, which is 'scratching your head'?" I forgot!)

However, there are a variety of options within your reach to improve your current practices related to the different flashpoints. Which ones strike you? You have to begin somewhere. One consolation is that everyone is wrestling with some of these same issues.

Although more research is needed to test the options presented, there are tentative solutions to the problems. Further, there is a lot of activity and discourse on these flashpoints, and the state of practice is constantly improving. After all, *look at the strides that have been made over the past few years in online administration procedures and the unethical and illegal strategies to increase response rates.*

Peter Pan Syndrome

With all that you and I both know about the 15 potential sources of evidence that can be used to evaluate teaching and the practices in your department, we can also make three incontrovertible predictions about your departmental decisions if nothing is done to improve current practices:

1. Your administrators will continue to make summative decisions about your faculty with or without the best information available.
2. Your administrators who make summative decisions with poorly developed measures will violate professional and, possibly, legal standards for personnel decisions and leave themselves open to litigation related to U.S. EEOC employment discrimination.
3. Your faculty members who are passionate about teaching will gather feedback from their students "by hook or by crook" and find data to help them improve their teaching.

In other words, if you exhibit the "Peter Pan syndrome" and do nothing to improve your evaluation practices, *your administrators and motivated faculty will make decisions they have to make regardless of the limitations they encounter and with or without the most valuable evidence* described in Flashpoints 1 and 2.

Top 10 Action Steps

The contribution of this problem-based writing (PBW) book rests on the value and usefulness of recommendations that you can convert into action. Without action, the recommendations are just dead words on the page or screen if you have the e-book. *Your takeaways are the concrete action steps you choose to implement to improve the current state of your teaching evaluation system.*

Here are the top 10 recommendations framed in terms of action steps:

1. Polish your student rating scale, but also start building additional sources of evidence to evaluate teaching effectiveness.
2. Match your highest quality sources to the specific formative, summative, and program decisions that need to be made.
3. Review current measures of teaching effectiveness with your faculty, and plan specifically how you can improve their quality.
4. Design an online administration system in-house or out-house with a vendor to conduct the administration and score reporting for your own student rating scale or the vendor's.
5. Standardize scale directions, administration procedures, and a narrow window for completion of the student rating scale and other measures of teaching effectiveness.
6. Select an appropriate combination of administrative and incentive strategies to increase online response rates to at least 60% for formative decisions and 80% for summative, and execute those strategies properly to assure those rates constantly increase and remain high year after year.
7. Use the total scale rating, instructor and course composite ratings, and/or subscale ratings across courses for summative decisions, but do *not* use global ratings.
8. Eliminate the "Neutral" option in rating scales; identify "Not Applicable" items during the field test and revise or discard to omit NA from the final scale; use the "Not Observed" or "Unable to Comment" option on observation scales; and code blanks, or nonresponses, with the midpoint value so scales will have same total number of item responses for all students.
9. Use criterion-referenced interpretations of anchor and item statistics, along with students' comments, to pinpoint areas for teaching improvement for formative decisions; use both criterion- and norm-referenced interpretations of total scale and subscale ratings for several courses and appropriate norm groups for contract renewal, merit pay, and promotion and tenure decisions.
10. Develop or adopt scales to measure teaching effectiveness in online courses, or use f2f scales with one or more subscale add-ons that address the uses of technology and other aspects of teaching that

are different for online courses. Administration of these scales would permit comparisons between f2f, online, and blended/hybrid courses.

Additional Flashpoints

If you found this PBW format useful to solve problems you face on the firing lines, please let me know. Also, send me other flashpoint ideas that I can add to my list when I consider another book on the topic. Only by thrashing out the flashpoints can we make progress on improving current practices. Since you don't have the time for thrashing and I do, send me your thoughts. I love thrashing. They will be most appreciated.

REFERENCES

Abrami, P. C. (2001). Improving judgments about teaching effectiveness using rating forms. In M. Theall, P. C. Abrami, & L. A. Mets (Eds.), *The student ratings debate: Are they valid? How can we best use them?* (New Directions for Institutional Research, No. 109) (pp. 59–87). San Francisco: Jossey-Bass.

Abrami, P. C., & d'Apollonia, S. (1990). The dimensionality of ratings and their use in personnel decisions. In M. Theall & J. Franklin (Eds.), *Student ratings of instruction: Issues for improving practice* (New Directions for Teaching and Learning, No. 43) (pp. 97–111). San Francisco: Jossey-Bass.

Abrami, P. C., & d'Apollonia, S. (1991). Multidimensional students' evaluations of teaching effectiveness—Generalizability of "$N = 1$" research: Comments on Marsh (1991). *Journal of Educational Psychology, 83,* 411–415.

Adams, C. M. (2012). Online measures of student evaluation of instruction. In M. E. Kite (Ed.), *Effective evaluation of teaching: A guide for faculty and administrators* (pp. 50–59). E-book retrieved on June 6, 2012, from the Society for the Teaching of Psychology website http://teachpsych.org/ebooks/evals2012/index .php.

Adams, M. J. D., & Umbach, P. D. (2012). Nonresponse and online student evaluations of teaching: Understanding the influence of salience, fatigue, and academic environments. *Research in Higher Education, 53*(5), 576–591. (DOI: 10.1007/ s11162-011-9240-5)

Addison, W. E., & Stowell, J. R. (2012). Conducting research on student evaluations of teaching. In M. E. Kite (Ed.), *Effective evaluation of teaching: A guide for faculty and administrators* (pp. 1–12). E-book retrieved on June 6, 2012, from the Society for the Teaching of Psychology website http://teachpsych.org/ebooks/evals2012/ index.php.

AERA (American Educational Research Association), APA (American Psychological Association), & NCME (National Council on Measurement in Education) Joint Committee on Standards. (1999). *Standards for educational and psychological testing.* Washington, DC: AERA.

Aleamoni, L. M. (1996). Why we do need norms of student ratings to evaluate faculty: Reaction to McKeachie. *Instructional Evaluation and Faculty Development, 16*(1–2), 18–19.

Algozzine, B., Beattie, J., Bray, M., Flowers, C., Gretes, J., Howley, L., Mohanty, G., & Spooner, F. (2004). Student evaluation of college teaching: A practice in search of principles. *College Teaching, 52*(4), 134–141.

Ali, D. L., & Sell, Y. (1998) *Issues regarding the reliability, validity and utility of student ratings of instruction: A survey of research findings.* Calgary: University of Calgary APC Implementation Task Force on Student Ratings of Instruction.

Allen, I. E., & Seaman, J. (2011). *Going the distance: Online education in the United States, 2011.* Babson Park, MS: Babson Survey Research Group. Retrieved on August 15, 2012, from http://www.onlinelearningsurvey.com/reports/goingthe distance.pdf.

Allison, P. D. (2000). Multiple imputation for missing data. *Sociological Methods & Research, 28*(3), 301–309.

American Evaluation Association. (2012). About us: Definition of evaluation. Retrieved on July 31, 2012, from http://www.eval.org/aboutus/organization/aboutus.asp.

Anderson, H. M., Cain, J., & Bird, E. (2005). Online student course evaluations: Review of literature and a pilot study. *American Journal of Pharmaceutical Education, 69*(1), Article 5, 34–43. (http://web.njit.edu/~bieber/pub/Shen-AMCIS 2004.pdf)

Anderson, J., Brown, G., & Spaeth, S. (2006). Online student evaluations and response rates reconsidered. *Innovate, 2*(6). Retrieved on June 3, 2012, from http://www.innovateonline.info/index.php?view=article&id=301.

Anderson, T., & Dron, J. (2011). Three generations of distance education pedagogy. *International Review of Research in Open and Distance Learning, 12,* 80–97.

APLU/Sloan National Commission on Online Learning. (2009, August). *Online learning as a strategic asset* (Vol. 1) (p. 41). Retrieved on July 17, 2012, from http://www.aplu.org/NetCommunity/Document.Doc?id=1877.

Apodaca, P., & Grad, H. (2005). The dimensionality of student ratings of teaching: Integration of uni- and multidimensional models. *Studies in Higher Education, 30,* 723–748.

Appling, S. E., Naumann, P. L., & Berk, R. A. (2001). Using a faculty evaluation triad to achieve evidenced-based teaching. *Nursing and Health Care Perspectives, 22,* 247–251.

Arreola, R. A. (2007). *Developing a comprehensive faculty evaluation system: A handbook for college faculty and administrators on designing and operating a comprehensive faculty evaluation system* (3rd ed.). Bolton, MA: Anker.

Arreola, R. A. (n.d.). Student ratings versus student evaluations of teaching. Retrieved on November 16, 2012, from http://www.cedanet.com/untitled/resource-links/arreola_sr_vs_se.pdf.

Ashe, L., & U.S. Equal Employment Opportunity Commission. (2007, May). Employment testing and screening: Recent developments in scored test case law. Retrieved on August 20, 2012, from http://eeoc.gov/eeoc/meetings/archive/5-16-07/testcase_ashe.html.

Avery, R. J., Bryan, W. K., Mathios, A., Kang, H., & Bell, D. (2006). Electronic course evaluations: Does an online delivery system influence student evaluations? *Journal of Economic Education, 37*(1), 21–37. (DOI: 10.3200/JECE.37.1.21-37)

Ballantyne, C. (2002, November). *Why survey online? A practical look at issues in the use of the Internet for surveys in higher education.* Paper presented at the annual meeting of the American Evaluation Association, Honolulu.

Ballantyne, C. (2003). Online evaluations of teaching: An examination of current practice and considerations for the future. In D. L. Sorenson & T. D. Johnson (Eds.), *Online student ratings of instruction* (New Directions for Teaching and Learning, No. 96) (pp. 103–112). San Francisco: Jossey-Bass.

Bangert, A. W. (2006). Identifying factors underlying the quality of online teaching effectiveness: An exploratory study. *Journal of Computing in Higher Education, 17*(2), 79–99. (DOI: 10.1007/BF03032699)

Bangert, A. W. (2008). The development and validation of the Student Evaluation of Online Teaching Effectiveness. *Computers in the Schools, 25*(1–2), 25–47. (DOI: 10.1080/07380560802157717)

Barnett, C. W., & Matthews, H. W. (2009). Teaching evaluation practices in colleges and schools of pharmacy. *American Journal of Pharmaceutical Education, 73*(6), Article 103.

Barnett, C. W., Matthews, H. W., & Jackson, R. A. (2003). A comparison between student ratings and faculty self-ratings of instructional effectiveness. *Journal of Pharmaceutical Education, 67*(4), Article 117.

Basow, S. A., & Martin, J. L. (2012). Bias in student evaluations. In M. E. Kite (Ed.), *Effective evaluation of teaching: A guide for faculty and administrators* (pp. 40–49). E-book retrieved on June 6, 2012, from the Society for the Teaching of Psychology website http://teachpsych.org/ebooks/evals2012/index.php.

Beattie, J., Spooner, F., Jordan, L., Algozzine, B., & Spooner, M. (2002). Evaluating instruction in distance learning classes. *Teacher Education and Special Education, 25*, 124–132.

Bennett, L., & Sid Nair, C. (2010). A recipe for effective participation rates for web-based surveys. *Assessment & Evaluation in Higher Education, 35*(4), 357–365.

Benton, S. L., & Cashin, W. E. (2012). *Student ratings of teaching: A summary of research and literature* (IDEA Paper No. 50). Manhattan, KS: The IDEA Center. Retrieved on April 8, 2012, from http://www.theideacenter.org/sites/default/files/idea-paper_50.pdf.

Benton, S. L., Webster, R., Gross, A., & Pallett, W. (2010a). *An analysis of IDEA Student Ratings of Instruction in traditional versus online courses* (IDEA Technical Report No. 15). Manhattan, KS: The IDEA Center.

Benton, S. L., Webster, R., Gross, A., & Pallett, W. (2010b). *An analysis of IDEA Student Ratings of Instruction using paper versus online survey methods* (IDEA Technical Report No. 16). Manhattan, KS: The IDEA Center.

Beran, T., Violato, C., & Kline, D. (2007). What's the "use" of student ratings of instruction for administrators? One university's experience. *Canadian Journal of Higher Education, 17*(1), 27–43.

Beran, T., Violato, C., Kline, D., & Frideres, J. (2005). The utility of student ratings of instruction for students, faculty, and administrators: A "consequential validity" study. *Canadian Journal of Higher Education, 35*(2), 49–70.

Berk, R. A. (1979). The construction of rating instruments for faculty evaluation: A review of methodological issues. *Journal of Higher Education, 50,* 650–669.

Berk, R. A. (Ed.). (1984). *A guide to criterion-referenced test construction.* Baltimore, MD: Johns Hopkins University Press.

Berk, R. A. (1986). A consumer's guide to setting performance standards on criterion-referenced tests. *Review of Educational Research, 56,* 137–172.

Berk, R. A. (1996). Standard setting: The next generation (Where few psychometricians have gone before!). *Applied Measurement in Education, 9,* 215–235.

Berk, R. A. (2005). Survey of 12 strategies to measure teaching effectiveness. *International Journal of Teaching and Learning in Higher Education, 17*(1), 48–62. (http://http://www.isetl.org/ijtlhe/pdf/IJTLHE8.pdf)

Berk, R. A. (2006). *Thirteen strategies to measure college teaching: A consumer's guide to rating scale construction, assessment, and decision making for faculty, administrators, and clinicians.* Sterling, VA: Stylus.

Berk, R. A. (2009a). Beyond student ratings: "A whole new world, a new fantastic point of view." *Essays on Teaching Excellence, 20*(1). (http://www.podnetwork.org/publications/teachingexcellence/05-06/V17,%20N2%20Berk.pdf)

Berk, R. A. (2009b). Using the 360-degree multisource feedback model to evaluate teaching and professionalism. *Medical Teacher, 31*(12), 1073–1080. (DOI: 10.3109/01421590802572775)

Berk, R. A. (2010). The secret to the "best" ratings from any evaluation scale. *Journal of Faculty Development, 24*(1), 37–39.

Berk, R. A. (2012, October 26). Top 5 flashpoints in the assessment of teaching effectiveness. *Medical Teacher,* 1–12. (Upcoming 2013 print issue). (DOI: 10.3109/0142159X.2012.732247) (http://informahealthcare.com/doi/abs/10.3109/0142159X.2012.732247)

Berk, R. A. (2013a). Face-to-face vs. online course evaluations: A "consumer's guide" to seven strategies. *MERLOT Journal of Online Learning and Teaching, 9*(1) (http://jolt/merlot.org/vol9no1/berk_0313.htm).

Berk, R. A. (2013b). Should global items on student rating scales be used for summative decisions? *Journal of Faculty Development, 27*(1), 57–61.

Berk, R. A. (in press). Top 20 strategies to increase the online response rates of student rating scales. *International Journal of Technology in Teaching and Learning, 8*(2).

Berk, R. A., Naumann, P. L., & Appling, S. E. (2004). Beyond student ratings: Peer observation of classroom and clinical teaching. *International Journal of Nursing Education Scholarship, 1*(1), 1–26.

Bracken, D. W., Timmreck, C. W., & Church, A. H. (Eds.). (2001). *The handbook of multisource feedback: The comprehensive resource for designing and implementing MSF processes.* San Francisco: Jossey-Bass.

Brandenburg, G. C., & Remmers, H. H. (1927). A rating scale for instructors. *Educational Administration and Supervision, 13*, 399–406.

Braskamp, L. A., & Ory, J. C. (1994). *Assessing faculty work: Enhancing individual and institutional performance.* San Francisco: Jossey-Bass.

Burton, W. B., Civitano, A., & Steiner-Grossman, P. (2012). Online versus paper evaluations: Differences in both quantitative and qualitative data. *Journal of Computing in Higher Education, 24*(1), 8–69. (DOI: 10.1007/s12528-012-9053-3)

Calderon, T. G., Gabbin, A. L., & Green, B. P. (1996). *Report of the committee on promoting evaluating effective teaching.* Harrisonburg, VA: James Madison University.

Carini, R. M., Hayek, J. C., Kuh, G. D., & Ouimet, J. A. (2003). College student responses to web and paper surveys: Does mode matter? *Research in Higher Education, 44*(1), 1–19. (DOI: 10.1023/A:1021363527731)

Carrier, N. A., Howard, G. S., & Miller, W. G. (1974). Course evaluations: When? *Journal of Educational Psychology, 66*, 609–613.

Cashin, W. E. (1989). *Defining and evaluating college teaching* (IDEA Paper No. 21). Manhattan, KS: The IDEA Center.

Cashin, W. E. (1990). *Student ratings of teaching: Recommendations for use* (IDEA Paper No. 22). Manhattan, KS: The IDEA Center.

Cashin, W. E. (1992). Student ratings: The need for comparative data. *Instructional Evaluation and Faculty Development, 12*(2), 1–6.

Cashin, W. E. (1994). Student ratings: Comparative data, norm groups, and non-comparative interpretations: Reply to Hativa and to Abrami. *Instructional Evaluation and Faculty Development,14*(1), 21–26.

Cashin, W. E. (1995). *Student ratings of teaching: The research revisited* (IDEA Paper No. 32). Manhattan, KS: The IDEA Center.

Cashin, W. E. (1996). Should student ratings be interpreted absolutely or relatively? Reaction to McKeachie. *Institutional Evaluation and Faculty Development, 16*(1–2), 14–19.

Cashin, W. E. (1999). Student ratings of teaching: Uses and misuses. In P. Seldin & Associates (Eds.), *Changing practices in evaluating teaching: A practical guide to improved faculty performance and promotion/tenure decisions* (pp. 25–44). Bolton, MA: Anker.

Cashin, W. E. (2003). Evaluating college and university teaching: Reflections of a practitioner. In J. C. Smart (Ed.), *Higher education: Handbook of theory and research* (pp. 531–593). Dordrecht, The Netherlands: Kluwer Academic Publishers.

Cashin, W. E., & Downey, R. G. (1992). Using global student ratings for summative evaluation. *Journal of Educational Psychology, 84*, 563–572.

Cashin, W. E., Downey, R. G., & Sixbury, G. R. (1994). Global and specific ratings of teaching effectiveness and their relation to course objectives: Reply to Marsh (1994). *Journal of Educational Psychology, 86*, 649–657.

Centra, J. A. (1976). The influence of different directions on student ratings of instruction. *Journal of Educational Measurement, 13*, 277–282.

Centra, J. A. (1993). *Reflective faculty evaluation: Enhancing teaching and determining faculty effectiveness.* San Francisco: Jossey-Bass.

Chase, M. (2007). Gender discrimination, higher education, and the seventh circuit: Balancing academic freedom with protections under Title VII, case note: *Farrell vs. Butler University. Wisconsin Women's Law Journal, 22*, 153–176. (http://hosted .law.wisc.edu/wjlgs/issues/2007-spring/chasenobanner.pdf)

Chen, Y., & Hoshower, L. B. (2003). Student evaluation of teaching effectiveness: An assessment of student perception and motivation. *Assessment &Evaluation in Higher Education, 28*(1), 71–88.

Chickering, A. W., & Gamson, Z. F. (1987). Seven principles for good practice in undergraduate education. *American Association of Higher Education Bulletin, 39*, 3–7. (http://www.uis.edu/liberalstudies/students/documents/sevenprinciples.pdf)

Cizek, G. J. (Ed.). (2001). *Setting performance standards: Concepts, methods, and perspectives.* Mahwah, NJ: Erlbaum.

Cohen, P. A. (1980). Using student rating feedback for improving college instruction: A meta-analysis of findings. *Research in Higher Education, 13*, 321–341.

Cohen, P. A. (1981). Student ratings of instruction and student achievement: A meta-analysis of multisection validity studies. *Review of Educational Research, 51*, 281–309.

Cohen, P. A., & McKeachie, W. J. (1980). The role of colleagues in the evaluation of teaching. *Improving College and University Teaching, 28*(4), 147–154.

Compora, D. (2003). Current trends in distance education: An administrative model. *Online Journal of Distance Learning Administration, 6*(2). Retrieved on July 10, 2012, from http://www.westga.edu/~distance/ojdla/summer62/com pora62.html.

Cook, C., Heath, F., & Thompson, R. (2000). A meta-analysis of response rates in web- or Internet-based surveys. *Educational and Psychological Measurement, 60*(6), 821–836. (DOI: 10.1177/00131640021970934)

Coren, S. (2001). Are course evaluations a threat to academic freedom? In S. E. Kahn & D. Pavlich (Eds.), *Academic freedom and the inclusive university* (pp. 104–117). Vancouver: University of British Columbia Press.

Creasman, P. A. (2012). *Considerations in online course design* (IDEA Paper No. 52). Manhattan, KS: The IDEA Center. Retrieved on August 15, 2012, from http:// www.theideacenter.org/sites/default/files/idea_paper_52.pdf.

Crews, T. B., & Curtis, D. F. (2011). Online course evaluations: Faculty perspective and strategies for improved response rates. *Assessment & Evaluation in Higher Education, 36*(7), 865–878.

d'Apollonia, S., & Abrami, P. C. (1997a). Navigating student ratings of instruction. *American Psychologist, 52*, 1198–1208.

d'Apollonia, S., & Abrami, P. C. (1997b). Scaling the ivory tower, Part 1: Collecting evidence of instructor effectiveness. *Psychology Teaching Review, 6*, 46–59.

d'Apollonia, S., & Abrami, P. C. (1997c). Scaling the ivory tower, Part 2: Student ratings of instruction in North America. *Psychology Teaching Review, 6,* 60–76.

DeSalvo, K. B., Fisher, W. P., Tran, K., Bloser, N., Merrill, W., & Peabody, J. (2006). Assessing measurement properties of two single-item general health measures. *Quality of Life Research, 15*(2), 191–201.

Deutskens, E., de Ruyter, K., Wetzels, M., & Oosterveld, P. (2004). Response rate and response quality of Internet-based surveys: An experimental study. *Marketing Letters, 15*(1), 21–36. (DOI: 10.1023/B:MARK.0000021968.86465.00)

DeVellis, R. F. (2012). *Scale development: Theory and applications* (3rd ed.). Thousand Oaks, CA: Sage.

Dolbier, C. L., Webster, J. A., McCalister, K. T., Mallon, M. W., & Steinhardt, M. A. (2005). Reliability and validity of a single-item measure of job satisfaction. *American Journal of Health Promotion, 19*(3), 194–198.

Dommeyer, C. J., Baum, P., & Hanna, R. W. (2002). College students' attitudes toward methods of collecting teaching evaluations: In-class versus on-line. *Journal of Education for Business, 78*(1), 5–11.

Dommeyer, C. J., Baum, P., Hanna, R. W., & Chapman K. S. (2004). Gathering faculty teaching evaluations by in-class and online surveys: Their effects on response rates and evaluations. *Assessment & Evaluation in Higher Education, 29*(5), 611–623. (DOI: 10.1080/0260293042000189171)

Donovan, J., Mader, C. E., & Shinsky, J. (2006). Constructive student feedback: Online vs. traditional course evaluations. *Journal of Interactive Online Learning, 5,* 283–296.

Drouin, M. (2012). What's the story on evaluations of online teaching? In M. E. Kite (Ed.), *Effective evaluation of teaching: A guide for faculty and administrators* (pp. 60–70). E-book retrieved on June 6, 2012, from the Society for the Teaching of Psychology website http://teachpsych.org/ebooks/evals2012/index.php.

Dunn-Rankin, P., Knezek, G. A., Wallace, S., & Zhang, S. (2004). *Scaling methods.* Mahwah, NJ: Erlbaum.

Edwards, M. R., & Ewen, A. J. (1996). *360 Feedback: The powerful new model for employee assessment and performance improvement.* New York: American Management Association (AMACOM).

Feldman, K. A. (1989a). The association between student ratings of specific instructional dimensions and student achievement: Refining and extending the synthesis of data from multisection validity studies. *Research in Higher Education, 30,* 583–645.

Feldman, K. A. (1989b). Instructional effectiveness of college teachers as judged by teachers themselves, current and former students, colleagues, administrators, and external (neutral) observers. *Research in Higher Education, 30,* 137–189.

Franklin, J. (2001). Interpreting the numbers: Using a narrative to help others read student evaluations of your teaching accurately. In K. G. Lewis (Ed.), *Techniques and strategies for interpreting student evaluations* (Special issue) (New Directions for Teaching and Learning, No. 87) (pp. 85–100). San Francisco: Jossey-Bass.

Franklin, J., & Theall, M. (1990). Communicating student ratings to decision makers: Design for good practice. In M. Theall & J. Franklin (Eds.), *Student ratings of instruction: Issues for improving practice* (Special issue) (New Directions for Teaching and Learning, No. 43) (pp. 75–93). San Francisco: Jossey-Bass.

Frey, P. W. (1976). Validity of student instructional ratings as a function of their timing. *Journal of Higher Education, 47,* 327–336.

Freyd, M. (1923). A graphic rating scale for teachers. *Journal of Educational Research, 8*(5), 433–439.

Gajic, A., Cameron, D., & Hurley, J. (2011). The cost-effectiveness of cash versus lottery incentives for a web-based, stated-preference community survey. *European Journal of Health Economics.* (DOI: 10.1007/s10198-011-0332-0)

Gamliel, E., & Davidovitz, L. (2005). Online versus traditional teaching evaluation: Mode can matter. *Assessment & Evaluation in Higher Education, 30*(6), 581–592. (DOI: 10.1080/02602930500260647)

Ginns, P., & Barrie, S. (2004). Reliability of single-item ratings of quality in higher education: A replication. *Psychological Reports, 95,* 1023–1030.

Gravestock, P., & Gregor-Greenleaf, E. (2008). *Student course evaluations: Research, models and trends.* Toronto: Higher Education Quality Council of Ontario. E-book retrieved on May 6, 2012, from http://www.heqco.ca/en-A/Research/Research%20Publications/Pages/Home.aspx.

Green, B. P., Calderon, T. G., & Reider, B. P. (1998). A content analysis of teaching evaluation instruments used in accounting departments. *Issues in Accounting Education, 13*(1), 15–30.

Griffin, A., & Cook, V. (2009). Acting on evaluation: Twelve tips from a national conference on student evaluations. *Medical Teacher, 31,* 101–104.

Guan, N. C., & Yusoff, M. S. B. (2011). Missing values in data analysis: Ignore or impute? *Education in Medicine Journal, 3*(1), e6–e11. (DOI: 10.5959/eimj .3.1.2011.0r1)

Hardy, N. (2002, April). *Perceptions of online evaluations: Fact and fiction.* Paper presented at the annual meeting of the American Educational Research Association, New Orleans, LA.

Hardy, N. (2003). Online ratings: Fact and fiction. In D. L. Sorenson & T. D. Johnson (Eds.), *Online student ratings of instruction* (New Directions for Teaching and Learning, No. 96) (pp. 31–38). San Francisco: Jossey-Bass.

Harrington, C. F., & Reasons, S. G. (2005). Online student evaluation of teaching for distance education: A perfect match? *The Journal of Educators Online, 2*(1), 1–12.

Harrison, P. D., Douglas, D. K., & Burdsall, C. A. (2004). The relative merits of different types of overall evaluations of teaching effectiveness. *Research in Higher Education, 45*(3), 311–323. (DOI: 10.1023/B:RIHE.0000019592.78752.da)

Hathorn, L., & Hathorn, J. (2010). Evaluation of online course websites: Is teaching online a tug-of-war? *Journal of Educational Computing Research, 42*(2), 197–217.

(http://baywood.metapress.com/openurl.asp?genre = article&issn = 0735-6331& volume = 42&issue = 2&spage = 197)

Hativa, N. (1993). Student ratings: A non-comparative interpretation. *Instructional Evaluation and Faculty Development, 13*(2), 1–4.

Hativa, N., & Raviv, A. (1993). Using a single score for summative teacher evaluation by students. *Research in Higher Education, 34*(5), 625–646. (DOI: 10.1007/ BF00991923) (http://link.springer.com/10.1007/BF00991923)

Heath, N., Lawyer, S., & Rasmussen, E. (2007). Web-based versus paper-and-pencil course evaluations. *Teaching of Psychology, 34*(4), 259–261. (DOI: 10.1080/ 00986280701700433)

Hong, P. C. (2008). Evaluating teaching and learning from students' perspectives in their classroom through easy-to-use online surveys. *International Journal of Cyber Society and Education, 1*(1), 33–48.

Hosie, R., Schibeci, R., & Backhaus, A. (2005). A framework and checklists for evaluating online learning in higher education. *Assessment & Evaluation in Higher Education, 35*(5), 539–553. (DOI: 10.1080/02602930500187097)

Hoyt, D. P., & Lee, E.-J. (2002). *Basic data for the revised IDEA system* (IDEA Technical Report No. 12). Manhattan, KS: Kansas State University Individual Development and Educational Assessment Center.

Hoyt, D. P., & Pallett, W. H. (1999). *Appraising teaching effectiveness: Beyond student ratings* (IDEA Paper No. 36). Manhattan, KS: Kansas State University Center for Faculty Evaluation and Development.

The IDEA Center (2008). Facilitating response rates in IDEA online. Manhattan, KS: The IDEA Center. Retrieved on March 5, 2012, from http://www.the ideacenter.org/OnlineResponseRates.

Johnson, T. D. (2001, September). *Online student ratings: Research and possibilities.* Invited plenary presented at the Online Assessment Conference, Champaign, IL.

Johnson, T. D. (2003). Online student ratings: Will students respond? In D. L. Sorenson & T. D. Johnson (Eds.), *Online student ratings of instruction* (New Directions for Teaching and Learning, No. 96) (pp. 49–60). San Francisco: Jossey-Bass.

Joint Committee on Standards for Educational Evaluation. (1994). *The program evaluation standards: How to assess systems of educational programs* (2nd ed.). Thousand Oaks, CA: Corwin Press.

Joint Committee on Standards for Educational Evaluation. (2009). *The personnel evaluation standards: How to assess systems for evaluating educators* (2nd ed.). Thousand Oaks, CA: Corwin Press.

Keig, L., & Waggoner, M. D. (1994). *Collaborative peer review: The role of faculty in improving college teaching* (ASHE-ERIC Higher Education Report, No. 2). Washington, DC: The George Washington University, Graduate School of Education and Human Development.

Kherfi, S. (2011). Whose opinion is it anyway? Determinants of participation in student evaluation of teaching. *Journal of Economic Education, 42*(1), 19–30.

Kite, M. E. (Ed.). (2012). *Effective evaluation of teaching: A guide for faculty and administrators.* E-book retrieved on June 6, 2012, from the Society for the Teaching of Psychology website http://teachpsych.org/ebooks/evals2012/index.php.

Knapper, C., & Cranton, P. (Eds.). (2001). *Fresh approaches to the evaluation of teaching* (New Directions for Teaching and Learning, No. 88). San Francisco: Jossey-Bass.

Laguilles, J. S., Williams, E. A., & Saunders, D. B. (2011). Can lottery incentives boost web survey response rates? Findings from four experiments. *Research in Higher Education, 52*(5), 537–553. (DOI: 10.1007/s11162-010-9203-2)

Layne, B. H., DeCristoforo, J. R., & McGinty, D. (1999). Electronic versus traditional student ratings of instruction. *Research in Higher Education, 40*(2), 221–232. (DOI: 10.1023/A:1018738731032)

Lepsinger, R., & Lucia, A. D. (2009). *The art and science of 360 feedback* (2nd ed.). San Francisco: Jossey-Bass.

Leung, D. Y. P., & Kember, D. (2005). Comparability of data gathered from evaluation questionnaires on paper through the Internet. *Research in Higher Education, 46*(5), 571–591. (DOI: 10.1007/s11162-005-3365-3)

Likert, R. (1932). A technique for the measurement of attitudes. *Archives of Psychology, 140*, 44–53.

Littman, A. J., White, E., Satia, J. A., Bowen, D. J., Kristal, A. R. (2006). Reliability and validity of two single-item measures of psychosocial stress. *Epidemiology, 17*(4), 398–403.

Liu, Y. (2006). A comparison of online versus traditional student evaluation of instruction. *International Journal of Instructional Technology and Distance Learning, 3*(3), 15–30.

Loveland, K. A. (2007). Student evaluation of teaching (SET) in web-based classes: Preliminary findings and a call for further research. *The Journal of Educators Online, 4*(2), 1–18.

Lucas, R. E., & Donnellan, M. B. (2012). Estimating the reliability of single-item life satisfaction measures: Results from four national panel studies. *Social Indicators Research, 105*(3), 323–331. (DOI: 10.1007/s11205-011-9783-z)

Marincovich, M. (1999). Using student feedback to improve teaching. In P. Seldin & Associates (Eds.), *Changing practices in evaluating teaching: A practical guide to improved faculty performance and promotion/tenure decisions* (pp. 45–69). Bolton, MA: Anker.

MarketTools. (2006). Zoomerang: Easiest way to ask, fastest way to know. Retrieved on July 17, 2012, from http://info.zoomerang.com.

Marsh, H. W. (1977). The validity of students' evaluations: Classroom evaluations of instructors independently nominated as best and worst teachers by graduating seniors. *American Educational Research Journal, 14*, 441–447. (DOI: 10.2307/1162341)

Marsh, H. W. (1980). The influence of student, course, and instructor characteristics in evaluations of university teaching. *American Educational Research Journal, 17,* 219–237. (DOI: 10.2307/1162484)

Marsh, H. W. (1984). Students' evaluations of university teaching: Dimensionality, reliability, validity, potential biases, and utility. *Journal of Educational Psychology, 76,* 707–754.

Marsh, H. W. (1987). Students' evaluations of university teaching: Research findings, methodological issues, and directions for future research. *International Journal of Educational Research, 11,* 253–388.

Marsh, H. W. (1991). Multidimensional students' evaluations of teaching effectiveness: A test of alternative higher-order structures. *Journal of Educational Psychology, 83,* 285–296. (DOI: 10.1037/0022-0663.83.2.285)

Marsh, H. W. (2001). Distinguishing between good (useful) and bad workloads on students' evaluations of teaching. *American Educational Research Journal, 38,* 183–212. (DOI: 10.3102/00028312038001183)

Marsh, H. W. (2007). Students' evaluations of university teaching: Dimensionality, reliability, validity, potential biases and usefulness. In R. P. Perry & J. C. Smart (Eds.), *The scholarship of teaching and learning in higher education: An evidence-based perspective* (pp. 319–383). Dordrecht, The Netherlands: Springer.

Marsh, H. W., & Hocevar, D. (1984). The factorial invariance of student evaluations of college teaching. *American Educational Research Journal, 21,* 341–366. (DOI: 10.2307/1162448)

Marsh, H. W., & Hocevar, D. (1991). Students' evaluations of teaching effectiveness: The stability of mean ratings of the same teachers over a 13-year period. *Teaching and Teacher Education, 7*(4), 303–314. (DOI: 10.1016/0742-051x(91)90001-6)

Marsh, H. W., Overall, J. U., & Kesler, S. P. (1979). Class size, student evaluations, and instructional effectiveness. *American Educational Research Journal, 16,* 57–69.

Marsh, H. W., & Roche, L. A. (1997). Making students' evaluations of teaching effectiveness effective: The critical issues of validity, bias, and utility. *American Psychologist, 52,* 1187–1197. (DOI: 10.1037/0003-066X.52.11.1187)

Marsh, H. W., & Roche, L. A. (2000). Effects of grading leniency and low workload on students' evaluations of teaching: Popular myths, bias, validity, or innocent bystanders? *Journal of Educational Psychology, 92*(1), 202–228. (DOI: 10.1037/0022-0663.92.1.202)

Mau, R. R., & Opengart, R. A. (2012). Comparing ratings: In-class (paper) vs. out of class (online) student evaluations. *Higher Education Studies, 2*(3). (DOI: 10.5539/hes.v2n3p55)

McGee, D. E., & Lowell, N. (2003). Psychometric properties of student ratings of instruction in online and on-campus courses. In D. L. Sorenson & T. D. Johnson (Eds.), *Online student ratings of instruction* (New Directions for Teaching and Learning, No. 96) (pp. 39–48). San Francisco: Jossey-Bass.

McKeachie, W. J. (1996). Do we need norms of student ratings to evaluate faculty? *Instructional Evaluation and Faculty Development, 15*(1–2), 14–17.

McKeachie, W. J. (1997). Student ratings: The validity of use. *American Psychologist, 52*(11), 1218–1225. (DOI: 10.1037/0003-066X.52.11.1218)

Me, I. M. (2003). Prehistoric teaching techniques in cave classrooms. *Rock & a Hard Place Educational Review, 3*(4), 10–11.

Me, I. M. (2005). Naming institutions of higher education and buildings after filthy rich donors with spouses who are dead or older. *Pretentious Academic Semi-Quarterly, 14*(4), 326–329.

Me, I. M., & You, W. U. V. (2005). Student clubbing methods to ensure teaching accountability. *Journal of Punching & Pummeling Evaluation, 18*(6), 170–183.

Morrison, R. (2011). A comparison of online versus traditional student end-of-course critiques in resident courses. *Assessment & Evaluation in Higher Education, 36*(6), 627–641.

Nathan, B. R., & Cascio, W. F. (1986). Introduction: Technical and legal standards. In R. A. Berk (Ed.), *Performance assessment: Methods and applications* (pp. 1–50). Baltimore, MD: Johns Hopkins University Press.

Netemeyer, R. G., Bearden, W. O., & Sharma, S. (2003). *Scaling procedures.* Thousand Oaks, CA: Sage.

Nilson, L. B. (2012). Time to raise questions about student ratings. In J. E. Groccia & L. Cruz (Eds.), *To improve the academy: Resources for faculty, instructional, and organizational development* (Vol. 31) (pp. 213–228). San Francisco: Jossey-Bass.

Norris, J., & Conn, C. (2005). Investigating strategies for increasing student response rates to online delivered course evaluations. *Quarterly Review of Distance Education, 6*(1), 13–29.

Nowell, J. B., Gale, L. R., & Handley, B. (2010). Assessing faculty performance using student evaluations of teaching in an uncontrolled setting. *Assessment & Evaluation in Higher Education, 35*(4), 463–475. (DOI: 10.1080/0260293090 2862875)

Nuhfer, E. B. (2010). A fractal thinker looks at student ratings. Retrieved on August 11, 2012, from http://profcamp.tripod.com/fractalevals10.pdf.

Nulty, D. (2008). The adequacy of response rates to online and paper surveys: What can be done? *Assessment & Evaluation in Higher Education, 33*(3), 301–314. (DOI: 10.1080/02602930701293231)

Oliver, R. L., & Sautter, E. P. (2005). Using course management systems to enhance the value of student evaluations of teaching. *Journal of Education for Business, 80*(4), 231–234.

Ory, J. C. (2001). Faculty thoughts and concerns about student ratings. In K. G. Lewis (Ed.), *Techniques and strategies for interpreting student evaluations* (Special issue) (New Directions for Teaching and Learning, No. 87) (pp. 3–15). San Francisco: Jossey-Bass.

Ory, J. C., & Ryan, K. (2001). How do student ratings measure up to a new validity framework? In M. Theall, P. C. Abrami, & L. A. Mets (Eds.), *The student ratings debate: Are they valid? How can we best use them?* (Special issue) (New Directions for Institutional Research, No. 109) (pp. 27–44). San Francisco: Jossey-Bass.

Otani, K., Kim, B. J., & Cho, J-Il. (2012). Student evaluation of teaching (SET) in higher education: How to use SET more effectively and efficiently in public affairs education. *Journal of Public Affairs Education, 18*(3), 531–544.

Parker, K., Lenhart, A., & Moore, K. (2011, August 28). The digital revolution and higher education. *Pew Internet and American Life Project.* Retrieved on July 10, 2012, from http://www.pewinternet.org/Reports/2011/College-presidents/Summary.aspx?view = all.

Peer, E., & Gamliel, E. (2011). Too reliable to be true? Response bias as a potential source of inflation in paper-and-pencil questionnaire reliability. *Practical Assessment, Research & Evaluation, 16*(9), 1–8. (http://pareonline.net/getvn.asp?v = 16%n = 9)

Peltier, J. W., Schibrowsky, J. A., & Drago, W. (2007). The interdependence of the factors influencing the perceived quality of the online learning experience: A causal model. *Journal of Marketing Education, 29,* 140–153. (DOI: 10.1177/0273475307302016)

Penny, A. R., & Coe, R. (2004). Effectiveness of consultation on student ratings feedback: A meta-analysis. *Review of Educational Research, 74,* 215–253.

Perrett, J. J. (2011). Exploring graduate and undergraduate course evaluations administered on paper and online: A case study. *Assessment & Evaluation in Higher Education,* 1–9. (DOI: 10.1080/02602938.2011.604123)

Primary Research Group. (2012, July). *The survey of distance learning programs in higher education, 2012–13 edition* (ISBN 1-57440-204-8). Retrieved on July 13, 2012, from http://www.primaryresearch.com/index.php.

Prunty, P. K. (2011). Bolstering student response rates for online evaluation of faculty. *Essays on Teaching Excellence, 23*(1). (http://podnetwork.org/publications/teachingexcellence.htm)

Quality Matters. (2007). Quality Matters rubric for evaluation of online and hybrid courses. Retrieved on July 17, 2012, from http://www.qmprogram.org/rubric.

Ravelli, B. (2000). Anonymous online teaching assessments: Preliminary findings. Retrieved on June 12, 2012, from http://www.edrs.com/DocLibrary/0201/ED445069.pdf.

Ravenscroft, M., & Enyeart, C. (2009). *Online student course evaluations. Strategies for increasing student participation rates.* Washington, DC: The Advisory Board Company. (http://tcuespot.wikispaces.com/file/view/Online + Student + Course + Evaluations + - + Strategies + for + Increasing + Student + Participation + Rates .pdf)

Remmers, H. H. (1928). The relationship between students' marks and students' attitudes toward instructors. *School and Society, 28,* 759–760.

Remmers, H. H. (1930). To what extent do grades influence student ratings of instructors? *Journal of Educational Research, 21*, 314–316.

Remmers, H. H., & Brandenburg, G. C. (1927). Experimental data on the Purdue Rating Scale for Instructors. *Educational Administration and Supervision, 13*, 519–527.

Renaud, R. D., & Murray, H. G. (2005). Factorial validity of student ratings of instruction. *Research in Higher Education, 46*(8), 929–953. (DOI: 10.1007/s11162-005-6934-6)

Roth, P. L. (1994). Missing data: A conceptual review for applied psychologists. *Personnel Psychology, 47*, 537–560.

Rothman, T., Romeo, L., Brennan, M., & Mitchell, D. (2011). Criteria for assessing student satisfaction with online courses. *International Journal for e-Learning Security (IJeLS), 1*(1–2), 27–32.

Rubin, D. B. (2004). *Multiple imputation for nonresponse in surveys*. Indianapolis: Wiley.

Sánchez-Fernández, J., Muñoz-Leiva, F., Montoro-Ríos, F. J., & Ibáñez-Zapata, J. A. (2010). An analysis of the effect of pre-incentives and post-incentives based on draws on response to web surveys. *Quality & Quantity, 44*(2), 357–373. (DOI: 10.1007/s11135-008-9197-4)

Sax, L., Gilmartin, S., & Bryant, A. (2003). Assessing response rates and non-response bias in web and paper surveys. *Research in Higher Education, 44*(4), 409–432. (DOI: 10.1023/A:1024232915870)

Scriven, M. (1991). *Evaluation thesaurus* (4th ed.). Newbury Park, CA: Sage.

Seldin, P. (1999). Current practices—good and bad—nationally. In P. Seldin & Associates (Eds.), *Changing practices in evaluating teaching: A practical guide to improved faculty performance and promotion/tenure decisions* (pp. 1–24). Bolton, MA: Anker.

Seldin, P. (2006). Building a successful evaluation program. In P. Seldin & Associates (Eds.), *Evaluating faculty performance: A practical guide to assessing teaching, research, and service* (pp. 1–19). Bolton, MA: Anker.

Seldin, P., & Associates. (Eds.). (2006). *Evaluating faculty performance: A practical guide to assessing teaching, research, and service*. Bolton, MA: Anker.

Sid Nair, C., & Adams, P. (2009). Survey platform: A factor influencing online survey delivery and response rate. *Quality in Higher Education, 15*(3), 291–296.

Sid Nair, C., Adams, P., & Mertova, P. (2008). Student engagement: The key to improving survey response rates. *Quality in Higher Education, 14*(3), 225–232.

Smalzried, N. T., & Remmers, H. H. (1943). A factor analysis of the Purdue Rating Scale for Instructors. *Journal of Educational Psychology, 34*, 363–367. (DOI: 10.1037/h0060532)

Sorenson, D. L., & Johnson, T. D. (Eds.). (2003). *Online student ratings of instruction* (New Directions for Teaching and Learning, No. 96). San Francisco: Jossey-Bass.

Sorenson, D. L., & Reiner, C. (2003). Charting the uncharted seas of online student ratings of instruction. In D. L. Sorenson & T. D. Johnson (Eds.), *Online student ratings of instruction* (New Directions for Teaching and Learning, No. 96) (pp. 1–29). San Francisco: Jossey-Bass.

Spooner, F., Jordan, L., Algozzine, B., & Spooner, M. (1999). Student ratings of instruction in distance learning and on-campus classes. *Journal of Educational Research, 92*, 132–140.

Stalmeijer, R. E., Dolmans, D. H., Wolfhagen, I. H., Peters, W. G., van Coppenolle, L., & Scherpbier, A. J. (2010). Combined student ratings and self-assessment provide useful feedback for clinical teachers. *Advances in Health Science Education, Theory, and Practice, 15*(3), 315–328.

Stehle, S., Spinath, B., & Kadmon, M. (2012). Measuring teaching effectiveness: Correspondence between students' evaluations of teaching and different measures of student learning. *Research in Higher Education, 53*(8), 888–904. (DOI: 10.1007/s11162-012-9260-9)

Stewart, I., Hong, E., & Strudler, N. (2004). Development and validation of an instrument for student evaluation of the quality of web-based instruction. *American Journal of Distance Education, 18*(3),131–150. (DOI: 0.1207/s15389286ajde 1803_2)

Stowell, J. R., Addison, W. E., & Smith, J. L. (2012). Comparison of online and classroom-based student evaluations of instruction. *Assessment & Evaluation in Higher Education, 37*(4), 465–473.

Strategy Group. (2011). *National strategy for higher education to 2030* (Report of the Strategy Group). Dublin, Ireland: Department of Education and Skills, Government Publications Office. Retrieved on July 17, 2012, from http://www.hea.ie/files/files/DES_Higher_Ed_Main_Report.pdf.

Streiner, D. L., & Norman, G. R. (2008). *Health measurement scales: A practical guide to their development and use* (4th ed.). New York: Oxford University Press.

Stufflebeam, D. L., & Shinkfield, A. J. (2007). *Evaluation theory, models, and applications*. San Francisco: Jossey-Bass.

Surgenor, P. W. G. (2011). Obstacles and opportunities: Addressing the growing pains of summative student evaluation of teaching. *Assessment & Evaluation in Higher Education*, 1–14, iFirst Article. (DOI: 10.1080/02602938.2011.635247)

Svinicki, M., & McKeachie, W. J. (2011). *McKeachie's teaching tips: Strategies, research, and theory for college and university teachers* (13th ed.). Belmont, CA: Wadsworth.

Tallent-Runnels, M. K., Thomas, J. A., Lan, W. Y., Cooper, S., Ahern, T. C., Shaw, S. M., & Liu, X. (2006). Teaching courses online: A review of the research. *Review of Educational Research, 76*(1), 93–135. (DOI: 10.3102/00346543076001093)

Theall, M. (1996). Who is Norm, and what does he have to do with student ratings? A reaction to McKeachie. *Instructional Evaluation and Faculty Development, 16*(1–2), 7–9.

Theall, M., Abrami, P. C., & Mets, L. A. (Eds.). (2001). *The student ratings debate: Are they valid? How can we best use them?* (New Directions for Institutional Research, No. 109). San Francisco: Jossey-Bass.

Theall, M., & Feldman, K. A. (2007). Commentary and update on Feldman's (1997) "Identifying exemplary teachers and teaching: Evidence from student ratings." In R. P. Perry & J. C. Smart (Eds.), *The teaching and learning in higher education: An evidence-based perspective* (pp. 130–143). Dordrecht, The Netherlands: Springer.

Theall, M., & Franklin, J. L. (1990). Student ratings in the context of complex evaluation systems. In M. Theall & J. L. Franklin (Eds.), *Student ratings of instruction: Issues for improving practice* (New Directions for Teaching and Learning, No. 43) (pp. 17–34). San Francisco: Jossey-Bass.

Theall, M., & Franklin, J. L. (2000). Creating responsive student ratings systems to improve evaluation practice. In K. E. Ryan (Ed.), *Evaluating teaching in higher education: A vision for the future* (Special issue) (New Directions for Teaching and Learning, No. 83) (pp. 95–107). San Francisco: Jossey-Bass.

Theall, M., & Franklin, J. L. (2001). Looking for bias in all the wrong places: A search for truth or a witch hunt in student ratings of instruction? In M. Theall, P. C. Abrami, & L. A. Mets (Eds.), *The student ratings debate: Are they valid? How can we best use them?* (New Directions for Institutional Research, No. 109) (pp. 45–56). San Francisco: Jossey-Bass.

Toepoel, V. (2012). Effects of incentives in surveys. In L. Gideon (Ed.), *Handbook of survey methodology for the social sciences* (pp. 209–223). New York: Springer. (DOI: 10.1007/978-1-4614-3876-2_13)

U.S. Code of Federal Regulations. (1978, August 25). *Uniform guidelines on employee selection procedures* (29 CFR part 1607, section 6A). Retrieved on November 11, 2012, from http://www.gpo.gov/fdsys/pkg/CFR-2011-title29-vol4/xml/CFR-2011-title29-vol4-part1607.xml.

U.S. Equal Employment Opportunity Commission (EEOC). (2010, September). Employment tests and selection procedures. Retrieved on August 20, 2012, from http://www.eeoc.gov/policy/docs/factemployment_procedures.html.

Van Selm, M., & Jankowski, N. W. (2006). Conducting online surveys. *Quality & Quantity, 40*(3), 435–456. (DOI: 10.1007/s11135-005-8081-8)

Venette, S., Sellnow, D., & McIntire, K. (2010). Charting new territory: Assessing the online frontier of student ratings of instruction. *Assessment & Evaluation in Higher Education, 35,* 101–115.

Wang, A. Y., & Newlin, M. H. (2000). Characteristics of students who enroll and succeed in psychology web-based classes. *Journal of Educational Psychology, 92,* 137–143.

Wang, M. C., Dziuban, C. D., Cook, I. J., & Moskal, P. D. (2009). Dr. Fox rocks: Using data-mining techniques to examine student ratings of instruction. In M. C. Shelley II, L. D. Yore, & B. Hand (Eds.), *Quality research in literacy and science education: International perspectives and gold standards* (pp. 383–398). Dordrecht, The Netherlands: Springer.

Wanous, J. P., & Hudy, M. J. (2001). Single-item reliability: A replication and extension. *Organizational Research Methods, 4*(4), 361–375. (DOI: 10.1177/1094 42810144003)

Wanous, J. P., Reichers, A. E., & Hudy, M. J. (1997). Overall job satisfaction: How good are single-item measures? *Journal of Applied Psychology, 82*(2), 247–252.

Waschull, S. B. (2001). The online delivery of psychology courses: Attrition, performance, and evaluation. *Computers in Teaching, 28,* 143–147.

Wei, C. C., Berkner, L., He, S., Lew, S., Cominole, M., Siegel, P., & Griffith, J. (2009). *2007–08 National Postsecondary Student Aid Study* (NPSAS: 08): *Student financial aid estimates for 2007–08, First look.* Washington, DC: U.S. Department of Education, National Center for Education Statistics. Retrieved on August 15, 2012, from http://nces.ed.gov/pubs2009/2009166.pdf.

Wines, W. A., & Lau, T. J. (2006). Observations on the folly of using student evaluations of college teaching for faculty evaluation, pay, and retention decisions and its implications for academic freedom. *William & Mary Journal of Women and the Law, 13*(1), 167–202. (http://works.bepress.com/cgi/viewcontent.cgi? article = 1007&context = terence_lau)

Wright, K. B. (2005). Researching Internet-based populations: Advantages and disadvantages of online survey research, online questionnaire authoring software packages, and web survey services. *Journal of Computer-Mediated Communication, 10*(3). Retrieved on July 17, 2012, from http://jcmc.indiana.edu/vol10/issue3/wright.html.

Yarbrough, D. B., Shulha, L. M., Hopson, R. K., & Caruthers, F. A. (2011). *The program evaluation standards: A guide for evaluators and evaluation users* (3rd ed.). Thousand Oaks, CA: Sage.

Yohannes, A. M., Dodd, M., Morris, J., & Webb, K. (2011). Reliability and validity of a single item measure of quality of life scale for adult patients with cystic fibrosis. *Health and Quality of Life Outcomes, 9,* 105. (DOI: 10.1186/1477-7525-9-105) (http://www.hqlo.com/content/9/1/105)

INDEX

Books by Ronald A. Berk

Humor as an Instructional Defibrillator
Evidence-Based Techniques in Teaching and Assessment

"He continues to inform and amuse readers about how he has used numerous strategies to help students enjoy various courses while learning the contents. Recommended."—***Choice***

Grab those paddles. Charge 300. Clear! "Ouch!" Now how do you feel? "Great!"

Humor can be used as a systematic teaching or assessment tool in your classroom and course website. It can shock students to attention and bring deadly, boring course content to life. Since some students have the attention span of goat cheese, we need to find creative online and offline techniques to hook them, engage their emotions, and focus their minds and eyeballs on learning. This book offers numerous techniques on how to effectively use humor in lectures and in-class activities, printed materials, course websites, and course tests and exams.

Thirteen Strategies to Measure College Teaching
A Consumer's Guide to Rating Scale Construction, Assessment, and Decision-Making for Faculty, Administrators, and Clinicians
Foreword by Michael Theall

"The humor is delightful and the information critical to understanding the process of evaluating assessment instruments. The University of North Texas has formed a committee to examine student evaluation forms as a first step to help measure overall teacher effectiveness. I have recommended that the other members purchase a copy."—***Paula Iaeger,*** GSA in the Office of the Provost and VP for Academic Affairs

"The evaluation of teaching is something that is done virtually wherever teaching itself is done. At too many places, though, it is done in a shallow, haphazard fashion. Ron Berk's book aims at evangelizing the rest of academia with the good news of how to do it right. This is ground that other well-respected academics have covered, but perhaps none aimed quite as much at the average faculty member.

For those who must develop student evaluation forms and other ratings instruments, the book contains invaluable information. Berk provides a step-by-step procedure for determining how the rating scales should be constructed, what questions (items) should asked, and what type of anchors (response choices) is appropriate. He provides examples of rating scales and items, both good and bad. Very importantly, he also provides clear instructions on how to field test the rating scale and how to determine its validity and reliability."—***International Journal for the Scholarship of Teaching and Learning***

22883 Quicksilver Drive
Sterling, VA 20166-2102

Subscribe to our e-mail alerts: www.Styluspub.com